# Figurative Language

## A Comprehensive Program

Multiple Meaning Words • Metaphors and Similes
Idioms and Proverbs • Riddles and Jokes • Clichés and Slang

**Second Edition**

**Kathleen A. Gorman-Gard, M.A., CCC-SLP**

 Super Duper® Publications • Greenville, South Carolina

© 2002 by Thinking Publications®
© 2008 by Super Duper® Publications

Super Duper® Publications grants limited rights to individual professionals to reproduce and distribute pages that indicate duplication is permissible. Pages can be used for instruction only and must include Super Duper® Publications' copyright notice. All rights are reserved for pages without the permission-to-reprint notice. No part of these pages can be reproduced in any form, electronic or mechanical, including photocopy, recording, or any information storage and retrieval system, without permission in writing from the publisher.

09   08                                                                 8   7   6   5   4   3

*Library of Congress Cataloging-in-Publication Data*

Gorman-Gard, Kathleen A., date
   Figurative language: a comprehensive program / Kathleen A. Gorman-Gard.—Second ed.
     p. cm.
   Includes bibliographical references.
   ISBN 978-1-888222-88-3 (pbk.)
     1. English language—Study and teaching—United States. 2. Figures of speech—Study and teaching—United States. 3. Children with disabilities—Education—United States. I. Title.

LB15767.G722 2002
808'.042'071—dc21
                                                                                        2001058356

*Printed in the United States of America*

*Cover design by Tim Davis*

*Illustrations by Kris Madsen and Kristin Kulig Sosalla*

*Cover Image: © Comstock Images® Corporation*

Super Duper® Publication
www.superduperinc.com
1-800-277-8737

For my parents,
Ray and Jenny Gorman,
for giving me roots and wings,
and for my two daughters,
Marissa and Erica,
for making my life busy and happy.


In Memorium:
For my great friend and colleague, Gwenn Goldstein,
who supported me personally and professionally
all the years I was privileged to know her.
She will be remembered fondly.

# About the Author

Kathleen received her BS and her MA in speech pathology from Kent State University. She is currently a speech-language pathologist for the Broward County Public School System, at Plantation High School in Plantation, Florida.

Kathleen has her Certificate of Clinical Competence (CCC) in speech pathology from the American Speech-Language-Hearing Association (ASHA) and has Florida teaching certification in speech-language pathology and English for Speakers of Other Languages (ESOL). In 1989, Kathleen was an infusion participant at the University of Florida for training in bilingual special education. Kathleen has worked extensively with adolescents for over 15 years. She has presented at numerous workshops on the topic of adolescent communication and has developed guidelines and activities for offering speech and language services for elective credit toward graduation. Her work has been published in *Advance* magazine and *Hearing Health*.

Kathleen is the mother of two active girls. She is a Girl Scout leader and "cookie mom" and spends most of her "free time" shuttling her daughters to and from gymnastics, birthday parties, and play dates. Kathleen and her daughters enjoy occasional trips to Walt Disney World and Sea World. Kathleen's personal interests include a variety of arts and crafts, sewing, stained glass, and home gardening. As an avid fan of home-and-garden programs, she takes great pride in her personal home improvement projects.

# Contents

Preface ............................................................................................................ vi

Introduction ...................................................................................................... 1

    What Is New in This Edition? ........................................................................ 3

    Who Is the Target Audience? ......................................................................... 3

    What Are the Goals? ..................................................................................... 4

    What Is Figurative Language? ....................................................................... 5

    How Should This Resource Be Used? ............................................................ 5

Activity Chapters ............................................................................................. 11

    Chapter 1: Multiple-Meaning Words ......................................................... 13

    Chapter 2: Metaphors and Similes ............................................................. 49

    Chapter 3: Idioms ..................................................................................... 81

    Chapter 4: Proverbs ................................................................................ 115

    Chapter 5: Humor (Riddles and Jokes) .................................................... 151

    Chapter 6: Clichés and Slang ................................................................... 179

References ...................................................................................................... 203

v

# Preface

It is hard to believe that nearly 10 years ago the first edition of *Figurative Language: A Comprehensive Program* was published. I considered my first book a significant accomplishment, but my work was far from complete. Almost immediately after it went to press, I began developing activities for what would become the second edition. I continued to work with high school students, and I believe they taught me at least as much as they learned from me. And there were those wonderfully satisfying moments when I knew that they really "got it." One memorable day, a student raced back from her English class to tell me that she was the only one in her class who knew what a simile was. Best of all, her class-mates thought she was "smart!" Her learning curve continued with her realization of the meaning of an expression her grandmother always said to her: "Tomorrow is but a promise." She had finally understood its true meaning. She triumphantly explained to me, "It's not a guarantee; anything can happen and you might not be here." It was a great moment for both of us. There were other moments, too, that gave me the determination to keep on writing and collecting ideas on scraps of paper to be developed into something more meaningful at a later time.

Although the basic framework for this book is the same as the first, I believe it is a much better product because there are so many more activities in this second edition. I spent a great deal of time "road-testing" the activities myself, rather than having colleagues field-test them for me. I am confi-dent that if you liked the first book, you'll love the second one and will enjoy having a whole new book full of fun figurative language activities.

First of all, I need to thank Nancy McKinley and Linda Schreiber at Thinking Publications for staying with me on this long-term project. Their patience while I "got things in order" was greatly appreciated. I would also like to thank Sarah Bennett, who field-tested this revision, and Dr. Marilyn Nippold, whom I have never met, but am grateful for her praises of my first book and her helpful cri-tique of my second book. Thank you to my brother Tom, who because of his recent return to college, helped me locate electronically some of the articles for my literature review, and to my mother, who actually came with me to the library to track down and copy the rest of them. Finally, thanks to the students who continue to learn right along side of me.

# Introduction

# What Is New in This Edition?

Like the first edition, the second edition of *Figurative Language: A Comprehensive Program* provides adolescents and adults with a variety of activities to develop their understanding and use of the following forms of figurative language:

- Multiple-meaning words
- Metaphors and similes
- Idioms
- Proverbs
- Humor (riddles and jokes)
- Clichés and slang

The six forms of figurative language that are targeted in this resource are the same as those in the first edition, but all of the activities in this second edition are new. Some activity types follow a similar format as in the first book, while others follow a brand-new format. For added convenience, answer keys and extension ideas are included as appropriate. Even so, as with the first edition, the activities are intended to generate discussion of figurative language, not to be used as mere paper-and-pencil worksheets.

# Who Is the Target Audience?

*Figurative Language* is intended for adolescents (ages 10–17) and adults who:

- Demonstrate communication or learning disabilities

- Have mild or moderate neurological impairments

- Demonstrate mild forms of autism

- Are learning English as a foreign language

Early research in figurative language showed that for the most part, children are engaged in formal operational thinking at about age 10 and above, when the experimental design of the task required children to explain the meaning of figurative language forms (Billow, 1975; Douglas and Peel, 1979; Gorham, 1956; Richardson and Church, 1959; Watts, 1950). Other studies that changed the experimental design of tasks found that children understood and produced a variety of figurative language forms well before they could explain them (Billow, 1975; Gardner, Winner, Bechhofer, and Wolf, 1978; Pollio and Pollio, 1974, 1979). For example, some studies found evidence of metaphoric detection in the preschool years (Gardner, Kircher, Winner, and Perkins, 1975; Winner, 1979). The idea that children must attain certain cognitive prerequisites prior to working on figurative language has fallen into disfavor in current research (Nippold, 1998; Vosniadou, 1987). Still, the relationship between cognition and the understanding and production of figurative language is not clear. For purposes of this

**Figurative Language**

book, age 10 is recommended as a general age for starting the program, as some of activities have explanation demands, and the content of the activities is most appropriate for adolescents and young adults.

Understanding and producing figurative language may well be a lifetime endeavor. Nippold (1998) points out that "language development has no clear point of completion" and further states, "it is difficult to identify any point in the lifespan when the process of language development is truly complete. Language development in adolescents is a gradual and protracted process and change can be difficult to observe" (p. 3). Some aspects of figurative language, such as proverb explanation, continue to develop well into adulthood (Nippold, Uhden, and Schwarz, 1997).

# What Are the Goals?

The overall goal of the *Figurative Language* program is to increase adolescents' and adults' understanding and production of six figurative language forms: multiple-meaning words, metaphors and similes, idioms, proverbs, humor (riddles and jokes), and clichés and slang. These forms of figurative language are not exhaustive, but they are representative of the figurative language forms encountered by adolescents in their daily academic and personal lives.

Multiple-meaning words may not be considered figurative language per se, but rather the building blocks for figurative language, thus they are included in this program. Students should demonstrate competence with multiple-meaning words before attempting more complicated forms. Other types of figurative language, such as hyperbole, irony, and onomatopoeia, are literary forms and are beyond the scope of this book.

Specific goals of this resource include:

- Understanding two or more meanings of multiple-meaning words

- Using a variety of meanings of multiple-meaning words

- Demonstrating comprehension of metaphors and similes

- Using metaphors and similes

- Identifying literal and figurative meanings of idioms

- Using idioms

- Showing an understanding of familiar fables

- Explaining proverbs found within fables and other short stories

- Demonstrating an understanding of riddles and jokes containing figurative language

- Using figurative language to create riddles and jokes

- Understanding of slang expressions

- Creating alternatives to clichés

# What Is Figurative Language?

Figurative language is language that is nonliteral, that is, language that has an intended meaning other than the meaning conveyed by the words stated. For example, the sentence *She hit the roof* has a nonliteral, figurative meaning of "She got upset." The intended meaning is different from the stated, literal meaning of the words, which would have her physically striking a roof. The English language is full of such figurative expressions. In fact, approximately two-thirds of the English language contains figurative expressions (Arnold and Hornett, 1990; Boatner and Gates, 1975). Furthermore, over one-third of "teacher talk" contains figurative expressions (Lazar, Warr-Leeper, Beel-Nicholson, and Johnson, 1989). Figurative language occurs at a rate of 10 instances in every 1,000 words in school textbooks (Evans and Gamble, 1988). Consequently, understanding and appropriate use of figurative language is necessary for academic and personal-social success (Nippold, 1985). Table I.1 (on page 6) provides definitions and examples of the six figurative language forms taught in the *Figurative Language* program.

The activities in this resource are based on figurative language research, the author's personal experiences working with adolescents with communication and learning disabilities, and information provided by the students themselves. Included in the program are commonly used forms of figurative language, appropriately targeted to several populations. Most importantly, the activities provide supportive contexts for correct, nonliteral interpretations of the targeted figurative language forms. Finally, the games and extension ideas in each chapter provide opportunities for carryover and transfer of the newly learned figurative language skills.

Use of supportive contexts and multiple-choice answers within some activities is modeled after current figurative language research (Evans and Gamble, 1988; Johnson, Ionson, and Torreiter, 1997; Nippold, 1998; Nippold, Allen, and Kirsch, 2000; Nippold and Haq, 1996). Cloze passages and using a cueing or "maze" variation, as described by Fry, Kress, and Fountoukidis (1993), is also incorporated at times.

# How Should This Resource Be Used?

There is a great deal of latitude in using this book. However, the activities are designed to generate discussion, not to be used as mere paper-and-pencil tasks. Direct instruction and discussion must

**Figurative Language**

| Table I.1 | *Figurative Language*'s Target Forms | |
|---|---|---|
| **Form** | **Definition** | **Examples** |
| **Multiple-Meaning Words** | Words that have more than one meaning. | *trip, spring, draw, ring, stall, bank, cover, rate* |
| **Metaphors and Similes** | Metaphors contain a topic and a vehicle that have a common or shared attribute (called the *ground);* similes are explicit metaphors that contain the grammatical markers *like, as,* or *as if.* | *John* (topic) *is the wind* (vehicle) *when he runs.*<br><br>and<br><br>*John runs like the wind.* |
| **Idioms** | Frozen figures of speech that can have both literal and nonliteral interpretations. | *He kicked the bucket.*<br>*Hold down the fort.* |
| **Proverbs** | Frozen figures of speech that teach a moral or lesson or that convey a warning; often quoted in fables. | *Waste not, want not.*<br>*Every cloud has a silver lining.* |
| **Humor** (Riddles and Jokes) | An ambiguity or a mismatch of ideas that must be resolved to appreciate its comic values; riddles and jokes have two or more interpretations condensed into one expression; riddles always use a question-and-answer format. | **Q.** *What has 4 wheels and flies?*<br>**A.** *A garbage truck.*<br><br>and<br><br>**JIM:** *I'm so hungry.*<br>**TIM:** *How hungry are you?*<br>**JIM:** *I'm so hungry, I could eat a horse.* |
| **Clichés and Slang** | Clichés are expressions that are overused; slang is street language and the current expressions of a particular group. | *good as gold; wonders never cease*<br>and<br>*chillin', hangin', for sure* |

*Introduction*

occur if students are to be successful with figurative language. Feel free to pick and choose activities as needed for your target populations. For example, if students are currently working on poetry in their English classes, then it would be advisable to skip ahead to metaphors and similes and to coordinate this with materials from their English class.

The activities on pages 18–23 and 25–28 in Chapter 1: Multiple-Meaning Words may be used as preintervention and postintervention activities to determine whether students are ready for more difficult figures. It is advisable to consider any level that is below 50% as unacceptable for continuation with Chapters 2–6. It may be necessary to use the multiple-meaning words activities in Chapter 1 as direct instruction, so that students understand the multiple meanings of words. This skill is necessary before students can be successful with the ambiguity of riddles and jokes or with comparing the attributes of the topic and vehicle of metaphors.

Keep in mind that mastery of a particular form of figurative language from Chapters 2–6 is not necessary before moving on to the next form. There appears to be no "all or none" mastery involved with understanding and producing figurative language, but rather a more gradual acquisition (Nippold, 1998). However, remember that it is advisable to work through the multiple-meaning words activities before conducting activities from the other five chapters, since multiple-meaning words form the basis of the other forms of figurative language.

When using an activity page with students, be sure everyone has access to a copy of the page. Either duplicate copies for students or have a copy displayed on an overhead projector. While students may be requested to complete a page on their own, be sure to review and discuss the items at some point to facilitate acquisition and reinforcement of the target concepts and skills.

The games described as the final activity within each of the six chapters should be attempted after students have been exposed to the other types of activities within the chapter. When playing the suggested games, include only items previously covered in the activities, instruction, or discussion. The purpose of the games is for students to practice using the targeted figurative language forms and to help them generalize this knowledge.

# Suggested Adaptations

## General Adaptations

Since this resource is designed to be used with a wide variety of students, activity pages may need to be adapted at times. Consider the following adaptations when attempting to make tasks easier or more challenging, depending on the needs of particular students.

1. To make items more salient to students, reread and/or paraphrase the activity aloud as students discuss and complete an activity page. Provide additional examples from students' experiences related to an activity page, and encourage students to offer their own explanations and examples.

**Figurative Language**

2. To scaffold student responses, ask yes/no or short-answer comprehension questions that lead to targeted responses.

3. To reduce the difficulty level of open-ended activities, turn a task into a cloze passage, multiple-choice, or matching activity. For example, when students are asked to give an example of a situation that is fitting to a particular proverb, give students a choice between two or three situations, rather than requesting they generate a scenario on their own.

4. To add more challenge to an activity, do not provide students with a copy of the activity sheet. Conducting an activity orally relies on students' listening comprehension skills and can add difficulty to a task.

5. To increase the difficulty level of multiple-choice, matching, or fill-in-the-blank tasks, remove the closed-ended options. For example, when students are presented with a sentence that contains a multiple-meaning word and told to circle the definition that explains how the word is being used in the given sentence, remove the multiple-choice option and simply ask students to define the given multiple-meaning word based on the sentence context alone.

6. To make the extension ideas more challenging, use vocabulary and figurative expressions that are found in students' academic and personal lives.

## Reading Adaptations

The activity pages within this resource have a fifth-grade readability level, according to the Fry (1977) formula. For students who have reading abilities at or below this level, or for those who have other reading difficulties (e.g., visual impairments or inability to read English fluently), one or more of the following adaptations could be made.

1. Pair strong readers with students who struggle with reading. Have the pairs help each other as they complete an activity page together.

2. Read the activity page aloud to students as the page is discussed and completed.

3. Make an audiotape recording of the activity page for students to listen to as they complete a page.

4. Provide an enlarged copy of an activity page to students who have visual difficulties.

5. Provide translations of the activity page into languages used by students who are learning English as a foreign language.

## Writing Adaptations

Keep in mind that written answers are not required from students in order to complete the activity pages. All activities can be done through a discussion format. However, the activity pages should still

8

*Introduction*

be used as a guide and can be helpful for recording important aspects of the class discussion. Recording answers also provides a future reference when reteaching a lesson. When students are required to write their responses, consider the following adaptations.

1. Have students work in pairs or small groups so that they can assist each other with spelling and grammar challenges.

2. Have students word-process their responses.

3. Enlist the assistance of a classroom paraprofessional so that students may dictate their responses to an adult.

4. Allow students learning English as a foreign language to provide their written answers in their native language.

The extension ideas provided throughout the chapters offer opportunities for collecting written samples of student work, which make excellent additions to student portfolios.

# Generalization

There are several ways to facilitate and to check for generalization of the figurative language skills taught in this program. A few of these techniques follow.

1. Use the extension ideas provided throughout the chapters. Be sure to tap into vocabulary and figurative language that is found in students' academic and personal lives.

2. Revisit activities from time to time to determine if knowledge and skills are being retained. Such repetition can facilitate acquisition of skills and check for generalization.

3. Communicate regularly with teachers and other adults in students' lives to inquire about students' understanding and use of figurative language. This is an excellent way to monitor student progress and to learn about vocabulary and figurative expressions that need continued attention.

9

# Activity Chapters

Chapter 1: Multiple-Meaning Words ...............................................................13

Chapter 2: Metaphors and Similes ................................................................49

Chapter 3: Idioms ........................................................................................81

Chapter 4: Proverbs ...................................................................................115

Chapter 5: Humor (Jokes and Riddles) .......................................................151

Chapter 6: Clichés and Slang .....................................................................179

# Multiple-Meaning Words

## Chapter 1

## What Are Multiple-Meaning Words?

Multiple-meaning words are words that have more than one meaning or referent. The meaning or referent vary based on how the word is used in a sentence. For example, depending on the surrounding context, the word *ring* can mean "an object worn on a finger" or "the sound a bell makes" or "a group of people performing illegal activities."

## Review of the Literature

It has been estimated that over 40% of the words in the English language have more than one meaning (Britton, 1978). Children encounter multiple-meaning words regularly in both spoken and written form (Johnson et al., 1997). For example, 72% of the 9,000 most frequently occurring words in one elementary reading series were found to have multiple meanings (Johnson and Pearson, 1984).

The ability to classify, define, and redefine multiple-meaning words is basic to the comprehension of figurative language (Wiig and Semel, 1984). Multiple-meaning words must be understood before a child can appreciate the ambiguity of jokes and riddles or the shared attributes of the topic and vehicle contained in metaphors and similes. In school, students must access intended meanings quickly and accurately in order to understand and respond to instructional discourse (Johnson et al., 1997). For success in subjects such as English and language arts, students must be able to detect ambiguities that arise from the multiple meanings of words (Wiig and Semel, 1980). The demands

**Figurative Language**

of interpreting multiple-meaning words (and other forms of figurative language) are staggering in the materials presented in high school history textbooks (Wiig and Semel, 1980).

There seems to be a link between word knowledge (which includes multiple meanings) and reading comprehension. Stahl, Richek, and Vandevier (1990) indicate that a lack of word knowledge impairs students' ability to read more challenging texts, with the gap between good and poor readers growing as students progress through their school years.

# Developmental Information

Comprehending multiple-meaning words requires knowledge of the different meanings of words and the ability to appreciate the linguistic context in which they occur (Nippold, Cuyler, and Braunbeck-Price, 1988). In general, high-frequency, concrete, literal word meanings are typically learned earlier than low-frequency, abstract, nonliteral word meanings (Mason, Kniseley and Kendall, 1979).

# How Can This Chapter Be Used?

## Analysis Forms

Chapter 1 is unique in that in addition to the activity pages, it also includes five reproducible analysis forms for monitoring students' understanding and use of multiple-meaning words. Pages 18–23 provide three different forms for analyzing students' comprehension of multiple-meaning words. (Form A, Form B, and Form C differ only in that they each target a different set of multiple-meaning words.) Direct students to read each word and the definitions that follow each word, circling the letters of all of the definitions that correctly apply to the given word. Remind students that more than one letter should be circled for each word. Use the Analysis section of the forms to show the number of words for which the student identified one, two, and three meanings. (Answer keys are provided for ease in scoring students' responses.) A percentage score can also be calculated for each, as shown.

Pages 25–28 provide two different forms for analyzing students' production of multiple-meaning words. Form A includes 10 multiple-meaning words for which students are directed to write sentences. Form B uses the same format as Form A, but it allows you to customize the form with 10 multiple-meaning words from students' academic and personal lives. Use the Analysis section of the forms to show the number of words for which the student generated one and two meanings.

These five analysis forms can be used to gather preintervention and postintervention information. They can be used with one or several students at a time; however, each student should have his or her own copy of the form to complete. In order to rule out the possibility that students are making errors

*Chapter 1: Multiple-Meaning Words*

due to an inability to read certain words, read the items aloud while students complete them. When using a form to collect baseline data or to document progress, limit the amount of assistance or discussion that is allowed while students are completing the items. Keep completed forms on record to document student progress over time.

If using the analysis forms for instruction, the following techniques are recommended: rereading items, paraphrasing, providing additional examples, asking students about their answers, and answering students' questions about the items. Using the forms to probe for student understanding may also help detect any error pattern that might exist. Ask students questions like "Why did you pick that answer?" and "Can you think of an action that that word can represent?" A great deal of discussion can be generated from these forms. Take care to direct the discussion so that students more fully understand the purpose of the activity. Refer to "Suggested Adaptations" (page 7) for additional ways to modify and present the analysis tasks.

# Activity Pages

There are four activities in Chapter 1. The activity pages can be used in any order. However, using the pages in the order in which they appear is recommended since they occur in a general progression from easier tasks to more difficult tasks. It is recommended that the card game described in Activity 4 be conducted after students have been exposed to the preceding activities within the chapter.

- **Activity 1** uses cloze sentences to help students demonstrate their understanding and use of multiple-meaning words. Students choose from the words provided at the top of each page to complete the sentences that follow. Two different versions—Form A and Form B—are provided, as is an answer key and extension ideas.

- **Activity 2** uses cloze stories to target multiple-meaning words. Students should be encouraged to pay attention to the context provided in each short story in order to choose the best word from a set of three choices to complete each blank. When a story has been completed, ask questions related to the information in the story to check for students' comprehension. Activity 2 includes Form A and Form B, as well as an answer key and extension ideas.

- **Activity 3** presents challenging and/or abstract multiple-meaning words in a matching activity. Explain to and demonstrate for students the process of starting with words that they may be most familiar with first in order to narrow down the number of definition options for the more difficult words. Form A and Form B are provided for Activity 3, as is an answer key and extension ideas.

- **Activity 4** presents directions and a word list for creating a card game to target students' understanding and use of multiple-meaning words. (Also consider using multiple-meaning words from the classroom curriculum and from students' daily lives for this activity.)

15

**Figurative Language**

For all four activities, encourage students to talk about the possible meanings of each multiple-meaning word as the tasks are discussed and completed. Also, direct students to read the tasks aloud to help them better recognize whether their response is accurate. Demonstrate techniques such as comparing and contrasting words using a graphic organizer (e.g., a Venn diagram), using context cues, and using reference materials (e.g., a dictionary) to figure out word meanings. Refer to "Suggested Adaptations" (page 7) for optional reading and writing activity modifications.

Table 1.1 includes lists of multiple-meaning words that might be useful when using the extension ideas described in this chapter. However, the extension activities will be even more effective when vocabulary from students' academic and personal lives is used.

Consider the activity pages as discussion guides rather than as paper-and-pencil tasks. Bridge discussions by talking about when students might encounter the given vocabulary items in their academic and/or personal lives.

*Chapter 1: Multiple-Meaning Words*

| Table 1.1 | Multiple-Meaning Words | | | | |
|---|---|---|---|---|---|
| angle | arch | arm | back | bag | ball |
| band | bank | bark | bat | bill | bit |
| block | bow | bowl | brush | can | case |
| catch | change | charge | check | clip | club |
| count | cup | date | deal | die | dock |
| down | draw | drive | duck | ear | egg |
| eye | fair | fall | fan | fat | fire |
| fit | flag | flat | fly | fresh | fry |
| gas | ground | grow | gum | guy | hail |
| hand | hatch | hawk | head | heart | hide |
| hold | horn | jack | jam | jar | jet |
| key | kid | kind | land | lap | last |
| lean | leave | lie | light | like | live |
| mail | march | mat | match | mean | mine |
| miss | model | nap | needle | note | pack |
| pad | palm | paper | part | pass | pet |
| pick | pitch | pool | pop | pound | press |
| pump | punch | rank | rash | reel | rest |
| ring | rock | roll | row | run | safe |
| sap | saw | scale | school | seal | season |
| set | shade | shop | shot | sign | size |
| slip | slug | smack | sock | soil | sow |
| space | spray | spring | stable | stamp | stand |
| steep | steer | stick | still | story | strike |
| strip | swing | tablet | tail | tap | tear |
| tick | tie | till | tip | tire | title |
| toast | tool | top | track | trunk | vice |
| wake | watch | water | wave | well | yard |

*Sources:* Dedrick and Lattyak (1984); Durkin and Manning (1989); Fry et al. (1993)

**Figurative Language**

# Multiple-Meaning Words—
# Comprehension Analysis
## Form A

Name: _____    Date: _____

### Directions

Multiple-meaning words are words that have two or more different definitions. Look at the words listed below. Each of these words has more than one meaning. Circle the letters of all the meanings that can define each word in bold.

HINT: There is more than one correct answer for each item. Be prepared to discuss your answers. Ask questions if you need assistance.

1. **bank**

   a. to take time off

   b. a place to save money

   c. the edge of a river

   d. to go on foot

   e. a metal tool

   f. to depend on

2. **break**

   a. the end of a segment

   b. time not spent working

   c. to pass along the way

   d. a stone

   e. to shatter

   f. to use in a kitchen

3. **draw**

   a. a shoe

   b. to climb

   c. a tie

   d. to take water from a source

   e. to waste time

   f. to sketch with a pen or pencil

4. **dump**

   a. to throw away

   b. a storage room

   c. to take time off

   d. a messy place

   e. a place for garbage

   f. a castle

18

**Figurative Language** © 2002 Thinking Publications
Duplication permitted for educational use only.

*Chapter 1: Multiple-Meaning Words*

5. **fly**

   a. a pocket

   b. a zipper on pants

   c. the total

   d. to travel by air

   e. a large animal

   f. an insect

6. **head**

   a. to argue

   b. a mark or spot

   c. a body part

   d. the top of something

   e. one who leads others

   f. a bed covering

7. **key**

   a. a tool to unlock something

   b. an answer

   c. a legend

   d. part of a tree

   e. a month

   f. a flavor

8. **light**

   a. low-calorie

   b. a fruit

   c. a chair

   d. not heavy

   e. useful

   f. a lamp

9. **match**

   a. a contest

   b. to look the same

   c. a heavy object

   d. a small stick with fire

   e. a cup for measuring

   f. a dance

10. **nail**

   a. to speak to

   b. to catch someone or something

   c. a body part on the tip of a finger

   d. a small metal spike

   e. to walk

   f. to jump up

---

**Analysis**

1 meaning identified: _____ out of 10 (_____%)

2 meanings identified: _____ out of 10 (_____%)

3 meanings identified: _____ out of 10 (_____%)

---

**Figurative Language** © 2002 Thinking Publications
Duplication permitted for educational use only.

**Figurative Language**

# Multiple-Meaning Words—
# Comprehension Analysis
## Form B

Name: _____  Date: _____

### Directions

Multiple-meaning words are words that have two or more different definitions. Look at the words listed below. Each of these words has more than one meaning. Circle the letters of all the meanings that can define each word in bold.

HINT: There is more than one correct answer for each item. Be prepared to discuss your answers. Ask questions if you need assistance.

1. **article**

   a. a piece of clothing

   b. a part of a car

   c. to shatter

   d. a story in a newspaper

   e. to admit

   f. a part of speech

2. **block**

   a. the main entrance

   b. concern for others

   c. a square piece of wood

   d. to stop or hinder

   e. a group of houses

   f. a metal spike

3. **bolt**

   a. to quickly run away

   b. a type of screw

   c. shoes

   d. to travel by air

   e. a large roll of fabric

   f. a place on a ship

4. **case**

   a. a piece of clothing

   b. a lawsuit

   c. to tap

   d. a box or container

   e. to laugh loudly

   f. to look for an illegal entry

20

**Figurative Language** © 2002 Thinking Publications
Duplication permitted for educational use only.

*Chapter 1: Multiple-Meaning Words*

5. **cover**
   a. the outside of a book
   b. an illness
   c. to hide or conceal
   d. to open
   e. a lid
   f. a piece of meat

6. **degree**
   a. an educational certificate
   b. an agreement
   c. a time of year
   d. a measure of temperature
   e. to take action
   f. an angle measurement

7. **disk**
   a. part of the spine
   b. a flying plate
   c. part of a book
   d. a computer device
   e. a printer
   f. a plan

8. **force**
   a. to move with strength
   b. an influential person or group
   c. a container
   d. a group of buildings
   e. a military or police unit
   f. to travel

9. **ground**
   a. to lift
   b. earth or dirt
   c. an electrical connection
   d. to take action
   e. mashed into pieces
   f. part of a plane

10. **interest**
    a. to pry open
    b. a pattern
    c. to pretend or act
    d. a fascination with something
    e. money earned
    f. a hobby

---

### Analysis

1 meaning identified: _____ out of 10 (_____%)

2 meanings identified: _____ out of 10 (_____%)

3 meanings identified: _____ out of 10 (_____%)

---

**Figurative Language** © 2002 Thinking Publications
Duplication permitted for educational use only.

**Figurative Language**

# Multiple-Meaning Words—
# Comprehension Analysis
## Form C

Name: _____  Date: _____

### Directions

Multiple-meaning words are words that have two or more different definitions. Look at the words listed below. Each of these words has more than one meaning. Circle the letters of all the meanings that can define each word in bold.

HINT: There is more than one correct answer for each item. Be prepared to discuss your answers. Ask questions if you need assistance.

1. **note**

   a. to see or observe

   b. a short letter

   c. an eraser

   d. a bridge

   e. a container

   f. to write down

2. **program**

   a. a television production

   b. to increase in size

   c. computer instructions

   d. to stop or hinder

   e. a performance

   f. fabric or cloth

3. **rattle**

   a. to follow

   b. a toy

   c. to annoy or upset

   d. to protect

   e. a craving for something

   f. to shake

4. **set**

   a. scenery on a stage

   b. to wiggle side to side

   c. to climb

   d. a matched group

   e. to place something

   f. to give money

22

**Figurative Language** © 2002 Thinking Publications
Duplication permitted for educational use only.

*Chapter 1: Multiple-Meaning Words*

5. **sharp**
   a. smart or quick-witted
   b. to operate
   c. nice-looking
   d. able to cut something
   e. to write with
   f. unusual or odd

6. **spring**
   a. a place in a barn
   b. a time of year
   c. a small stream of water
   d. a metal coil
   e. to catch
   f. a point

7. **sweep**
   a. to pretend or act
   b. to complain or argue
   c. a body part
   d. to use a broom
   e. to win all games in a series
   f. to extend gracefully

8. **trip**
   a. a telephone call
   b. to find something
   c. a vacation or an outing
   d. to fall
   e. pale in color
   f. to start or trigger something

9. **trunk**
   a. part of a bike
   b. an elephant's nose
   c. animal fur
   d. part of a tree
   e. the engine of a car
   f. the back of a car

10. **will**
    a. a boy's name
    b. a legal document
    c. to excuse
    d. a position or job
    e. to walk in line
    f. to intend to do something

---

### Analysis

1 meaning identified: _____ out of 10 (_____%)

2 meanings identified: _____ out of 10 (_____%)

3 meanings identified: _____ out of 10 (_____%)

---

**Figurative Language** © 2002 Thinking Publications
Duplication permitted for educational use only.

Figurative Language

# Multiple-Meaning Words—
# Comprehension Analysis
## Answer Key

**Form A (pgs 18–19)**

1. **bank**—b, c, f
2. **break**—a, b, e
3. **draw**—c, d, f
4. **dump**—a, d, e
5. **fly**—b, d, f

6. **head**—c, d, e
7. **key**—a, b, c
8. **light**—a, d, f
9. **match**—a, b, d
10. **nail**—b, c, d

**Form B (pgs 20–21)**

1. **article**—a, d, f
2. **block**—c, d, e
3. **bolt**—a, b, e
4. **case**—b, d, f
5. **cover**—a, c, e

6. **degree**—a, d, f
7. **disk**—a, b, d
8. **force**—a, b, e
9. **ground**—b, c, e
10. **interest**—d, e, f

**Form C (pgs 22–23)**

1. **note**—a, b, f
2. **program**—a, c, e
3. **rattle**—b, c, f
4. **set**—a, d, e
5. **sharp**—a, c, d

6. **spring**—b, c, d
7. **sweep**—d, e, f
8. **trip**—c, d, f
9. **trunk**—b, d, f
10. **will**—a, b, f

24

*Chapter 1: Multiple-Meaning Words*

# Multiple-Meaning Words—
# Production Analysis
## Form A

Name: _____ Date: _____

### Directions

Multiple-meaning words are words that have two or more different definitions. For each word listed, think of two different meanings. State the two meanings by giving definitions or by using the word in two different sentences. Be prepared to discuss your answers. An example has been provided to get you started. Ask questions if you need assistance.

---

**Example**

**strike**

   a. *The umpire said, "Strike 2!"*

   b. *He will strike the desk with his fist.*

---

1. **gas**

   a. _____

   b. _____

2. **bowl**

   a. _____

   b. _____

3. **miss**

   a. _____

   b. _____

4. **run**

   a. _____

   b. _____

**Figurative Language** © 2002 Thinking Publications
Duplication permitted for educational use only.

25

**Figurative Language**

5. **shot**

   a. _____

   b. _____

6. **flag**

   a. _____

   b. _____

7. **game**

   a. _____

   b. _____

8. **post**

   a. _____

   b. _____

9. **racket**

   a. _____

   b. _____

10. **dart**

   a. _____

   b. _____

---

## Analysis

1 meaning generated: _____ out of 10 (_____%)

2 meanings generated: _____ out of 10 (_____%)

*Chapter 1: Multiple-Meaning Words*

# Multiple-Meaning Words— Production Analysis

## Form B

Name: _____  Date: _____

### Directions

Multiple-meaning words are words that have two or more different definitions. For each word listed, think of two different meanings. State the two meanings by giving definitions or by using the word in two different sentences. Be prepared to discuss your answers. An example has been provided to get you started. Ask questions if you need assistance.

---

**Example**

**change**

    a. *Change your clothes.*

    b. *I've got 20 cents in change in my pocket.*

---

1. _ _ _ _ _ _ _ _ _ _

    a. _____

    b. _____

2. _ _ _ _ _ _ _ _ _ _

    a. _____

    b. _____

3. _ _ _ _ _ _ _ _ _ _

    a. _____

    b. _____

**Figurative Language** © 2002 Thinking Publications
Duplication permitted for educational use only.

**Figurative Language**

4. _ _ _ _ _ _ _ _ _ _

    a. _____

    b. _____

5. _ _ _ _ _ _ _ _ _ _

    a. _____

    b. _____

6. _ _ _ _ _ _ _ _ _ _

    a. _____

    b. _____

7. _ _ _ _ _ _ _ _ _ _

    a. _____

    b. _____

8. _ _ _ _ _ _ _ _ _ _

    a. _____

    b. _____

9. _ _ _ _ _ _ _ _ _ _

    a. _____

    b. _____

10. _ _ _ _ _ _ _ _ _ _

    a. _____

    b. _____

---

## Analysis

1 meaning generated: _____ out of 10 (_____%)

2 meanings generated: _____ out of 10 (_____%)

*Chapter 1: Multiple-Meaning Words*

# Activity 1—Cloze Sentences
## Form A

Name: _____     Date: _____

### Directions

Read the following sentences. From the words listed at the top of the page, choose the best word to complete each sentence. Each word will get used several times. Be prepared to discuss your answers. Ask questions if you need assistance.

**cup**        **pick**        **club**        **stamp**

1. I can drink from a _____.

2. I _____ my foot on the ground.

3. He belongs to the drama _____ at school.

4. I need a _____ of sugar.

5. They go to the _____ to dance.

6. _____ out some clothes to wear to school.

7. The soccer team won the World _____.

8. I have a _____ on my hand from the fair.

9. He uses a _____ to style his hair.

10. I _____ my hands together to pick up the sand.

11. The older kids tried to _____ on the new student.

12. I put a _____ on the letter.

13. The caveman used a _____ to beat open the shell.

14. He used a rubber _____ to make the card.

15. He can _____ a pocket without anyone seeing him.

16. She uses The _____ to keep her car from being stolen.

**Figurative Language** © 2002 Thinking Publications
Duplication permitted for educational use only.

29

**Figurative Language**

## grow      tie      hand      date      fall

17. The baby will _____ if he drinks a lot of formula.

18. The leaves change in the _____.

19. He hurt his _____ yesterday.

20. The plants will _____ if they receive water and sunlight.

21. He wore a shirt and _____ to dinner.

22. I can _____ a tricky knot.

23. We went on a _____ to the movies.

24. The interest on his savings account will _____ each month.

25. The _____ on the calendar says August 16.

26. The game ended in a _____.

27. He decided to _____ a beard.

28. The boat went over the water _____.

29. They are going to "_____ the knot" next weekend.

30. _____ in your homework on time.

31. They set the _____ for their wedding.

32. He took the _____ for the crime.

33. Give her a _____ with those books.

34. She made _____ bars for the picnic.

35. Try not to _____ off the edge.

36. _____ me the newspaper, please.

*Chapter 1: Multiple-Meaning Words*

# Activity 1—Cloze Sentences
## Form B

Name: _____ Date: _____

## Directions

Read the following sentences. From the words listed at the top of the page, choose the best word to complete each sentence. Each word will get used several times. Be prepared to discuss your answers. Ask questions if you need assistance.

### strike    band    punch    safe

1. The umpire called, "_____!"

2. The waist _____ on my pants is elastic.

3. He was _____ at home plate.

4. I like to drink fruit _____.

5. You keep money in a _____.

6. He was in the marching _____.

7. She wears a head _____ all the time.

8. I tried to _____ a hole in the wall.

9. _____ a match to light the fire.

10. I feel _____ in school.

11. The unhappy workers will go out on _____.

12. She cannot _____ that note very well.

13. I need to use the hole _____.

14. It is _____ to drink the water now.

15. The papers are held together with a rubber_____.

16. I need to _____ out for lunch.

**Figurative Language** © 2002 Thinking Publications
Duplication permitted for educational use only.

31

**Figurative Language**

| top | fair | row | back | toast |
| --- | --- | --- | --- | --- |

17.  All the children were standing in a _____.

18.  The student who received the best score is at the _____ of the class.

19.  _____ the car into the driveway.

20.  Put the _____ on that jar.

21.  Let's drink a _____ to the new year.

22.  I need the video _____ by Monday.

23.  That was his third knockout in a _____.

24.  That girl has _____ skin.

25.  Sit in the last _____.

26.  We learned how to _____ a boat at camp last summer.

27.  I know how to make _____.

28.  I want to buy a new _____ to match my pants.

29.  The _____ of the chair is rounded at the top.

30.  He says that the teacher's grading system is not _____.

31.  She was the _____ of the town.

32.  Anything leftover tomorrow is _____ game.

33.  He has a bad _____, so he can't lift heavy things.

34.  Put the cookies on _____ of the counter.

35.  She wants to go to the county _____.

36.  The sun is so hot today she is going to _____!

# Activity 1—Cloze Sentences
## Answer Key

**Form A (pgs 29–30)**

| | | |
|---|---|---|
| 1. cup | 13. club | 25. date |
| 2. stamp | 14. stamp | 26. tie |
| 3. club | 15. pick | 27. grow |
| 4. cup | 16. club | 28. fall |
| 5. club | 17. grow | 29. tie |
| 6. pick | 18. fall | 30. hand |
| 7. cup | 19. hand | 31. date |
| 8. stamp | 20. grow | 32. fall |
| 9. pick | 21. tie | 33. hand |
| 10. cup | 22. tie | 34. date |
| 11. pick | 23. date | 35. fall |
| 12. stamp | 24. grow | 36. hand |

**Form B (pgs 31–32)**

| | | |
|---|---|---|
| 1. strike | 13. punch | 25. row |
| 2. band | 14. safe | 26. row |
| 3. safe | 15. band | 27. toast |
| 4. punch | 16. punch | 28. top |
| 5. safe | 17. row | 29. back |
| 6. band | 18. top | 30. fair |
| 7. band | 19. back | 31. toast |
| 8. punch | 20. top | 32. fair |
| 9. strike | 21. toast | 33. back |
| 10. safe | 22. back | 34. top |
| 11. strike | 23. row | 35. fair |
| 12. strike | 24. fair | 36. toast |

Figurative Language

# Activity 1—Cloze Sentences
## Extension Ideas

1. Have students explain or write their own sentences for the multiple-meaning words in Activity 1. Students can record written examples in a journal.

2. Have students write their own cloze sentences for a new set of multiple-meaning words. (As an option, have students also include hints for the word that completes a sentence. See the example below, which demonstrates how hints might be used.) Have students exchange papers and then read and complete each other's sentences.

   *Someday I will _____ to be an adult.*
   *(HINT: get older and larger)*

*Chapter 1: Multiple-Meaning Words*

# Activity 2—Cloze Stories
## Form A

Name: _____ Date: _____

### Directions

Read the following short stories. Choose the best word to complete each blank from the words listed below it. Use the surrounding words and facts to help you. Be prepared to discuss your answers. Ask questions if you need assistance.

**1** The game was tied 0 to 0 with no _____ in the ninth inning. The next
hits / steps / space

batter stepped up to the _____. The first pitch was a _____.
plate / stand / shelf                                        seed / mind / ball

The next pitch was a _____ run. The 1 to 0 victory earned the
sweet / cold / home

batter a place in the annual all- _____ game.
star / player / out

---

**2** The elegant couple went to the _____ together. The _____
ball / field / store                    club / band / pack

began to play their favorite song. As they were about to _____ onto
play / sit / step

the dance floor, the girl broke her shoe. The couple decided to _____
rest / pick / bore

instead of dance that evening. They found a lovely _____ to sit at on
stair / table / rock

the patio, underneath the stars.

**Figurative Language** © 2002 Thinking Publications
Duplication permitted for educational use only.

35

**Figurative Language**

**3**  I took my car into the repair _____. The mechanic said, "I will have to
house / flat / **shop**

adjust the fan _____ and _____ the battery cable." He also
**belt** / bolt / nut          paint / twirl / **ground**

said he would be charging me a _____ price since the repairs were minor.
**fair** / cold / home

He finished by saying, "Of _____, that's just a guess. The final bill
best / **course** / stamp

could be much higher. You never know what I'm gonna find once I get started."

---

**4**  My grandmother can _____ any kind of flower in the world. She has
eat / stay / **grow**

the largest _____ of roses I've ever seen. She loves to _____
lump / **bed** / road                                    move / **dig** / send

her plants around in the _____ from year to year. She's strong and
**yard** / foot / frame

she digs up the _____ by herself. Some people call her Mrs. Greenthumb.
**ground** / leaves / water

---

**5**  I went to _____ to contest a speeding ticket I got on my moped. I told
spot / timer / **court**

the _____ that my bike doesn't travel as fast as I was accused of going.
**judge** / man / teacher

He said he would rule on the _____ as soon as he looked at my bike.
thing / **case** / can

He looked at my moped and dismissed the _____, but said I could not
**fine** / take / date

use the bike anymore because it was not _____ to ride it on the road.
**safe** / feel / see

36

*Chapter 1: Multiple-Meaning Words*

# Activity 2—Cloze Stories
## Form B

Name: _____ Date: _____

### Directions

Read the following short stories. Choose the best word to complete each blank from the words listed below it. Use the surrounding words and facts to help you. Be prepared to discuss your answers. Ask questions if you need assistance.

**1** Tennis is my favorite sport to _____. I get out on the _____

soap / **play** / seat          floor / stairs / **court**

every chance I get. I can _____ a ball almost 90 miles per hour. My

**hit** / see / take

_____ is so powerful that I can ace almost anyone. I can also put a fast

head / foot / **serve**

_____ on the ball when I return a serve.

**spin** / hat / card

**2** My uncle is constructing the four- _____ building in town. First, he

plant / pen / **story**

had to lay the cement _____. Next, he had to cut the _____

dirt / **block** / plane          **boards** / grounds / parks

for the frame. Finally, he had to _____ the drywall by hand. I hope

**finish** / stop / send

that when his work is complete, it will _____ the inspection of his

take / **pass** / help

supervisors.

Figurative Language © 2002 Thinking Publications
Duplication permitted for educational use only.

**Figurative Language**

**3** The police were trying to _____ the suspects. They had just tried to
freeze / tail / end

rob a small _____ on the edge of town. The suspects were easy to
tank / boat / bank

_____ because they were running. One even tried to _____
spot / tide / wake                                                    kick / seen / scale

a fence, but he got stuck. Finally, the police were able to _____ up
face / round / stake

all of the suspects.

**4** I want to _____ out a video to watch tonight. I would like to see one
pick / step / sale

with a really good _____. Or perhaps a mystery with a suspenseful
hide / story / mad

_____. I also enjoy romance, when the _____ is made in
plot / same / food                                    stars / moon / match

heaven. It's always nice to _____ home and relax while watching a
catch / stay / learn

good show.

**5** I don't like the _____ of that machine. It's too _____ and
air / staple / sound                              loud / tall / round

it moves and shakes. I can't _____ anything that makes a lot of noise.
stand / see / cry

Maybe you could _____ it off for a while. My ears would appreciate
stop / send / switch

the _____.
break / brake / cold

*Chapter 1: Multiple-Meaning Words*

# Activity 2—Cloze Stories
## Answer Key

**Form A (pgs 35–36)**

1. hits, plate, ball, home, star

2. ball, band, step, rest, table

3. shop, belt, ground, fair, course

4. grow, bed, move, yard, ground

5. court, judge, case, fine, safe

**Form B (pgs 37–38)**

1. play, court, hit, serve, spin

2. story, block, boards, finish, pass

3. tail, bank, spot, scale, round

4. pick, story, plot, match, stay

5. sound, loud, stand, switch, break

Figurative Language

# Activity 2—Cloze Stories
## Extension Ideas

1. Have students write their own cloze stories. Direct students to pick four multiple-meaning words and make up four related sentences that comprise a short story so that each sentence includes one of the chosen multiple-meaning words. (Table I.1, on page 17, provides dozens of multiple-meaning words that could be used for this activity.) Then have students write out the sentences, leaving blanks for the multiple-meaning words. Have students either write the four multiple-meaning words at the top of the page or provide multiple-choice options for each of the blanks. Once students have created their stories, have them exchange papers with a partner and then read and complete each other's stories.

2. Use paragraphs from students' textbooks or other narrative assignments to create additional cloze paragraphs to use with students. Write or word-process a set of related sentences, omitting several multiple-meaning words. Have students fill in the blanks to complete the paragraphs.

# Activity 3—
# Defining Multiple-Meaning Words
## Form B

Name: _____   Date: _____

### Directions

There are three corresponding definitions for each of the multiple-meaning words listed on this activity page. Fill in the blanks under each word with the appropriate definitions. Use each definition only one time. Cross off the definitions as you write them in the blanks. Be prepared to discuss your answers. Ask questions if you need assistance.

**1**

| reason | spurt | track |
|--------|-------|-------|
| _____ | _____ | _____ |
| _____ | _____ | _____ |
| _____ | _____ | _____ |

| | | |
|--------|-------|-------|
| an excuse | a sudden growth | an animal trail |
| a song on a CD | an explanation | to jump forward |
| extra energy | to think | a place for car racing |

Figurative Language © 2002 Thinking Publications
Duplication permitted for educational use only.

43

**Figurative Language**

## 2

| ring | turn | seal |
|------|------|------|
| _____ | _____ | _____ |
| _____ | _____ | _____ |
| _____ | _____ | _____ |
| to rotate or flip | a sea animal | to close tightly |
| a stamp | a circular line | to chime |
| to go against | to shake a bell | to change direction |

## 3

| subject | sheet | register |
|---------|-------|----------|
| _____ | _____ | _____ |
| _____ | _____ | _____ |
| _____ | _____ | _____ |
| a topic | to enroll | a bed covering |
| a person | a class | a cash holder |
| a list of names | a page with music | a piece of paper |

## 4

| rod | game | guard |
|-----|------|-------|
| _____ | _____ | _____ |
| _____ | _____ | _____ |
| _____ | _____ | _____ |
| a long stick | to protect | willing to |
| a basketball player | something fun to play | animals |
| a watchman | a pole for fishing | part of the eye |

*Chapter 1: Multiple-Meaning Words*

# Activity 3—
# Defining Multiple-Meaning Words
## Answer Key

**Form A (pgs 41–42)**

1. **act**
   part of a play
   to perform
   a law

   **base**
   the bottom of a lamp
   headquarters
   alkaline

   **body**
   the main part of a letter
   a physical being
   an organization

2. **character**
   a letter
   a person in a play
   a personality

   **stall**
   to waste time
   a place in a barn
   to break down

   **break**
   to shatter
   time off
   to exceed

3. **count**
   nobility
   to matter
   to add numbers

   **form**
   to shape
   a document
   a type

   **ground**
   earth
   mashed into pieces
   the lowest floor

4. **block**
   a group of homes
   to stop
   a football move

   **chain**
   metal links
   multiple stores
   a series

   **condition**
   a rule
   to treat hair
   the state of

**Form B (pgs 43–44)**

1. **reason**
   an explanation
   an excuse
   to think

   **spurt**
   a sudden growth
   to jump forward
   extra energy

   **track**
   a song on a CD
   a place for car racing
   an animal trail

45

**Figurative Language**

2.  **ring**
    to shake a bell
    a circular line
    to chime

    **turn**
    to rotate or flip
    to change direction
    to go against

    **seal**
    a sea animal
    to close tightly
    a stamp

3.  **subject**
    a topic
    a class
    a person

    **sheet**
    a piece of paper
    a page with music
    a bed covering

    **register**
    to enroll
    a cash holder
    a list of names

4.  **rod**
    a long stick
    part of the eye
    a pole for fishing

    **game**
    something fun to play
    willing to
    animals

    **guard**
    a watchman
    to protect
    a basketball player

46

# Activity 3— Defining Multiple-Meaning Words

## Extension Ideas

1. Have students write sentences using two or more meanings for the multiple-meaning words used in Activity 3. Students can write their examples in a journal or on the production analysis form provided on pages 27–28. For example,

   **burn**

   *The fire fighters will let the fire burn itself out.*

   *I usually burn the food when I do the cooking.*

2. Search magazine and newspaper headlines and advertisements for multiple-meaning words. Clip out these examples and present them to students. Discuss the intended meanings of the multiple-meaning words and talk about the context that is provided (or assumed) that makes the meanings clear.

**Figurative Language**

# Activity 4— Multiple-Meaning Words Card Game

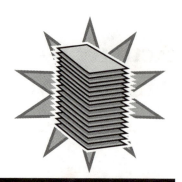

### Directions

Create a multiple-meaning words card deck. Choose from the words provided below, or use words from students' classroom curriculum and daily lives. For each example, write the word on one side of a 3" × 5" index card. If possible, have students help create the card deck.

Group students into two teams. Place the deck facedown in the center of a table. Have teams take turns choosing the top card from the deck and saying the word aloud to the other team. The responding team must then state at least two meanings of the given word. If the responding team is successful, they keep the card. If the responding team is not successful, the card should be returned to the bottom of the deck. The team with the most cards at the end wins.

NOTE: As another option, write the words on one set of cards and the meanings on another set of cards (being sure to include each word two or more times, depending on the number of meanings being used for each). Then use the two decks to play a classic game of Memory by having students match words to their meanings.

| bank | cover | band | ground | dart | break |
|---|---|---|---|---|---|
| degree | fall | article | rattle | draw | disk |
| strike | chain | date | dump | force | punch |
| condition | gas | fly | rod | safe | character |
| bowl | head | interest | stall | fair | bolt |
| miss | key | program | pick | reason | run |
| light | sweep | toast | tie | shot | match |
| sharp | top | count | flag | nail | will |
| row | trip | form | note | stamp | back |
| turn | post | set | cup | act | seal |
| racket | spring | grow | base | subject | block |
| hand | body | register | trunk | club | ring |
| guard | game | track | case | sheet | spurt |

48

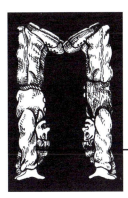

# Metaphors and Similes

## Chapter 2

## What Are Similes and Metaphors?

Similes and metaphors have embodied the majority of research in regard to figurative language. In some instances, *metaphor* has even been used synonymously with *figurative language.* Both similes and metaphors allow us to find similarities between things that at first appear to be very different. *Metaphor* comes from the Greek word *metaphora* meaning "to carry over." Generally, a metaphor conveys ideas that cannot be literally expressed, more effectively communicates the vividness of an idea, and offers great teaching value (Readence, Baldwin, and Rickelman, 1983). For instance, the metaphor "The stars are jewels against a velvet curtain," vividly expresses the beauty of a star-filled sky. A metaphor is also a figure of speech that is a comparison. It has a topic and a vehicle. The topic and the vehicle have a common or shared attribute, which is called the *ground.* The topic in the previous metaphor is "the stars" and the vehicle is "jewels." The ground is their shared brilliance. *Simile* comes from the Latin word *similis,* meaning "like." The difference between a metaphor and a simile is largely structural. Similes are an explicit variation of a metaphor and usually contain one of three grammatical markers: *like, as,* or *as if.* For example, the simile *He's like the wind* contains the marker *like.* The metaphor *He's the wind* contains no marker.

Similes and metaphors appear more frequently in written form than in spoken form. They also appear more frequently in the content areas of literature, history, and science. Historically, writers, such as William Shakespeare and Emily Dickinson, and scientists, such as Charles Darwin, frequently employed the use of similes and metaphors in their writings. Philosophers, such as Aristotle and Socrates, used metaphoric language to explain their theories. Aristotle is even attributed with having said, "The greatest thing by far is to master the metaphor" (Schaefer, 1975). Today, poets, recording artists, and advertisers all rely heavily on similes and metaphors to express their ideas. Because of the

**Figurative Language**

pervasiveness of similes and metaphors throughout history, as well as in modern-day use, their understanding and use is critical to successful communication.

# Review of the Literature

Much of the research related to similes and metaphors from the 1950s through the 1970s has been discounted, or refined by more sensitive experimental tasks. Even so, nearly as many questions seem to appear from the subsequent studies, and some questions about the nature of metaphoric competence in young children may never be fully answered. In the 1960s and 1970s, developmental, stage, and processing theories emerged (Asch and Nerlove, 1960; Billow, 1975, 1977; Douglas and Peel, 1979; Winner, 1979). Figurative language development was seen as a reflection of the growth of underlying logical operations (Billow, 1975, 1977; Gardner et al., 1978).

During the last two decades, there has been a sizable increase in the quantity and quality of research on metaphors. In the 1980s and 1990s, a number of studies began to look at specific or unique linguistic populations, such as people with learning disabilities or hearing impairments, nonnative English speakers, and African Americans (Baechle and Lian, 1990; Dahany, 1986; Iran-Nejad, Ortony, and Rittenhouse, 1981; Jones and Stone, 1989; Lee and Kamhi, 1990; Ortony, Turner, and Larson-Shapiro, 1985a, 1985b; Seidenberg and Bernstein, 1986; Smith, Schloss, and Israelite, 1986; Towne and Entwisle, 1993; Wiig, 1985). Their unique needs and abilities have just begun to become addressed through research. Today, studies focus on the structure and complexity of similes and metaphors, and the context in which they are used, as well as other factors, such as background knowledge (Baechle and Lian, 1990; Evans and Gamble, 1988; Jones and Stone, 1989; Lee and Kamhi, 1990; Nippold, 1985, 1998; Nippold, Leonard, and Kail, 1984; O'Brien and Martin, 1988; Vosniadou, 1987).

The purpose of this book is not to take a particular position about the nature of metaphoric competence or to add to the current philosophical debate of whether this competence is developmental or stagelike in nature, when it first appears in children, or what exactly constitutes a metaphor. What is essential for using this chapter is how it applies to increasing the understanding and production of similes and metaphors in adolescents and adults. Therefore, the most pertinent aspects of the research for this particular population will be presented. For a comprehensive review of the literature, see Nippold (1998) and Vosniadou (1987).

# Developmental Information

Early studies in figurative language research determined that the metaphor was a literary embellishment that had a nonessential role in communication (Watts, 1950). Explanation of metaphors was

50

believed to be heavily influenced by the development of cognitive abilities. Piaget (1926) advanced a framework that indicated children must largely be in the stage of formal operational thinking, ages 10–12, in order to competently explain metaphors. These views have fallen under heavy attack and into disfavor in current research. Subsequent studies show that the explanation task demands masked the child's ability to understand and use metaphors. It was also believed during this time period that similes were slightly easier to explain than metaphors, due to their explicit nature (Nippold, 1998; Vosniadou, 1987).

In applying the pertinent research related to typical development, comprehension activities are assumed to be easier than production or explanation activities. Also, because of their explicit nature, similes are assumed to be easier to comprehend, produce, and explain than metaphors. After direct instruction, students older than 10 years of age should be able to complete the activities that require metaphor production and explanation (Seidenberg and Bernstein, 1986).

# How Can This Chapter Be Used?

There are five activities in Chapter 2. It is recommended that you begin with Activity 1, as the activities progress from easier to more challenging tasks. However, use discretion and feel free to pick and choose activities to meet the particular needs of each student. It is also recommended that the card game described in Activity 5 be conducted after students have been exposed to the preceding activities within the chapter. Because similes are easier to understand and produce than metaphors, cue students to use *like, as,* or *as if* when they have difficulty producing metaphors. Prompt students to list the characteristics that the topic and the vehicle have in common and then compare them to each other.

- **Activity 1** uses a multiple-choice format to help students demonstrate their understanding of similes. In addition, students are asked to extend their knowledge of similes by producing some on their own. Form A and Form B are provided for Activity 1, as is an answer key and extension ideas.

- **Activity 2** uses a multiple-choice format to target comprehension of metaphors. Activity 2 includes Form A and Form B, an answer key, and extension ideas.

- **Activity 3** delves deeper into students' understanding of metaphors by asking them to explain why a comparison in a metaphor is being made. To make the task easier, students are first asked to turn the metaphor into a simile. Form A and Form B are provided for Activity 3, as are extension ideas.

- **Activity 4** presents a challenging task that asks students to rank possible meanings related to metaphor and simile comparisons. Activity 4 includes Form A, Form B, an answer key, and extension ideas.

**Figurative Language**

- **Activity 5** presents directions and a list of similes and metaphors for creating a card game to target students' understanding and use of these linguistic concepts. (Also consider using similes and metaphors from the classroom curriculum and from students' daily lives for this activity.)

For all five activities, encourage students to talk about the possible meanings of each simile or metaphor as the tasks are discussed and completed. Also, direct students to read the tasks aloud to help themselves better recognize whether a response is accurate. Demonstrate the use of context cues, graphic organizers (e.g., a Venn diagram), visual representations (e.g., drawings), and reference materials (e.g., a thesaurus) to show students how to understand and use similes and metaphors. For added convenience, Table 2.1 describes excellent, acceptable, and unacceptable use of similes and metaphors and Table 2.2 provides a hierarchy of metaphor types. Refer to "Suggested Adaptations" (page 7) for optional reading and writing activity adaptations.

Consider the activity pages as discussion guides rather than as paper-and-pencil tasks. Bridge discussions by talking about when students might encounter the given similes and metaphors in their academic and/or personal lives.

| Table 2.1 | Use of Similes and Metaphors | | |
|---|---|---|---|
| **Example** | **Responses** | | |
| | **Excellent** | **Acceptable** | **Unacceptable** |
| **Comparing a lake to glass** | *The lake was as clear as glass.* *The lake is as smooth as glass.* *The lake is clear glass early in the morning.* | *The lake is like a glass because you can see your reflection in it.* | *I used a glass to get some water from the lake.* (Student doesn't compare the two words, but uses them in one sentence.) |
| **Comparing a barbed-wire fence to a porcupine** | *The barbed-wire fence is as sharp as a porcupine.* *The barbed-wire fence is a pointy porcupine.* *The barbed-wire fence was a porcupine on the boy's leg.* | *The boy jumping over the fence said it felt like a porcupine.* | *The barbed-wire fence and the porcupine are both sharp.* (Student doesn't compare the two words, but uses them in one sentence.) |

| Table 2.2 | Hierarchy of Metaphor Types | |
|---|---|---|
| **Level** | **Description** | **Examples** |
| **1—Predictive Metaphors** | Contain one topic and one vehicle. The vehicle is usually concrete and tangible. The ground is the shared or common attribute. | *The boy was a mouse.* *His hair was a nest.* *The swimmer was a fish.* |
| **2—Perceptual Metaphors** | Show a visual resemblance between two items. | *The moon was a diamond in the sky.* *Aunt Marie was a marshmallow walking down the road.* |
| **3—Psychological Metaphors** | Express an emotion, mental state, or personality characteristics. | *His dog's rage was a thunderous storm.* *The nurse was medicine to the injured man.* |
| **4—Proportional Metaphors** | Include two topics—one stated and one unstated— in analogous relationship to the two vehicles, which are both stated. | *Ann's arm was a tomato that squirted juice.* (Unstated topic: Her arm was bleeding badly) *The quarterback was a vine that had no grapes.* (Unstated topic: The quarterback couldn't play well) |

*Sources:* Nippold (1985); Nippold et al. (1984)

**Figurative Language**

# Activity 1—Understanding and Using Similes
## Form A

Name: _____ Date: _____

### Directions

Similes are sentences that compare two ideas or things using the words *like, as,* or *as if.* Many times similes contain multiple-meaning words. Read the following similes and circle the best meaning of the multiple-meaning word used in the simile. Then write your own simile using the multiple-meaning word. Be prepared to discuss your answers. Ask questions if you need assistance.

1. **She's as sweet as a kitten.**

   a. *sweet* refers to:  a taste / a kind personality / beloved

   b. Write your own simile using the word *sweet:* _____

   _____

   _____

2. **The baby's skin feels as soft as cotton.**

   a. *soft* refers to:  smoothness / fluffiness / easy

   b. Write your own simile using the word *soft:* _____

   _____

   _____

54

**Figurative Language** © 2002 Thinking Publications
Duplication permitted for educational use only.

*Chapter 2: Metaphors and Similes*

3. **The edge of the paper was as sharp as a knife.**

    a. *sharp* refers to:  keen / able to cut something / mild

    b. Write your own simile using the word *sharp:* _____

    _____

    _____


4. **The union strike was like letting the air out of a balloon.**

    a. *strike* refers to:  hitting something / stopping working / swinging a bat and
    missing the ball

    b. Write your own simile using the word *strike:* _____

    _____

    _____


5. **Her skin looked like it was cut from plastic.**

    a. *cut* refers to:  to be taken off the team / to use a knife / to be watered down

    b. Write your own simile using the word *cut:* _____

    _____

    _____


6. **His hair was as wild as a bird's nest.**

    a. *wild* refers to:  an untamed animal / fun / not orderly or neat

    b. Write your own simile using the word *wild:* _____

    _____

    _____

**Figurative Language** © 2002 Thinking Publications
Duplication permitted for educational use only.

55

**Figurative Language**

# Activity 1—Understanding and Using Similes
## Form B

Name: _____     Date: _____

### Directions

Similes are sentences that compare two ideas or things using the words *like*, *as*, or *as if*. Many times similes contain multiple-meaning words. Read the following similes and circle the best meaning of the multiple-meaning word used in the simile. Then write your own simile using the multiple-meaning word. Be prepared to discuss your answers. Ask questions if you need assistance.

1. **The trip to New York was like medicine.**

    a. *trip* refers to:  a vacation / to fall down / to trigger or set off

    b. Write your own simile using the word *trip:* _____

    _____

    _____

2. **The carnival was like a bad date.**

    a. *date* refers to:  a day on a calendar / a social appointment /a time in the past

    b. Write your own simile using the word *date:* _____

    _____

    _____

**Figurative Language** © 2002 Thinking Publications
Duplication permitted for educational use only.

56

*Chapter 2: Metaphors and Similes*

 **She was a magnet to bad luck.**

She was attractive.     Many unfortunate things happened to her.

 **The building was a soldier in the city.**

The building was army green.     The building was sturdy and tall.

 **The fighter plane was an angry bee buzzing in the sky.**

The plane forcefully attacked its target.     There was a bee inside the plane's cockpit.

 **The TV was a cheap babysitter.**

The TV entertained the children.     The TV was inexpensive.

 **Her ankles were rubber bands in those high-heeled shoes.**

Her ankles were broken.     She couldn't walk well in high heels.

 **The kitchen was the heart of their home.**

The oven made the kitchen warm.     Important events took place in the kitchen.

**Figurative Language**

# Activity 2—Understanding Metaphors
## Answer Key

### Form A (pgs 60–61)

1. Her skirt lifted up in the wind.
2. Roses smell sweet and fragrant.
3. Pine trees are sharp and prickly.
4. The tree shows the changing of seasons.
5. The principal is in charge.
6. Flamingos are balanced and graceful.
7. My dog barks at strangers.
8. My mother keeps us safe.
9. The game kept her busy.
10. The classroom is cold.

### Form B (pgs 62–63)

1. She enjoys gardening.
2. The team surrounded the building.
3. Our teacher has students who don't behave.
4. Her bedroom was a mess.
5. Many unfortunate things happened to her.
6. The building was sturdy and tall.
7. The plane forcefully attacked its target.
8. The TV entertained the children.
9. She couldn't walk well in high heels.
10. Important events took place in the kitchen.

*Chapter 2: Metaphors and Similes*

**3**

*Metaphor*—His **feet** are two **tugboats.**

*Simile*—His feet are _____ two tugboats.

His feet are two tugboats because _____

_____

**4**

*Metaphor*—The lights in the **room** made it a **desert.**

*Simile*—The lights in the room made it _____ a desert.

The lights in the room made it a desert because _____

_____

**5**

*Metaphor*—That **child** was an **octopus** in the toy store.

*Simile*—That child was _____ an octopus in the toy store.

That child was an octopus in the toy store because _____

_____

**6**

*Metaphor*—**Fear** was a **noose** around my neck.

*Simile*—Fear was _____ a noose around my neck.

Fear was a noose around my neck because _____

_____

**7**

*Metaphor*—The **baby's coo** was **music** to my ears.

*Simile*—The baby's coo was _____ music to my ears.

The baby's coo was music to my ears because _____

_____

**Figurative Language** © 2002 Thinking Publications
Duplication permitted for educational use only.

**Figurative Language**

# Activity 3—Explaining Similes and Metaphor
## Extension Ideas

1. Using the metaphors from Activity 3, have students substitute a similar or related word for the second bold word in each. For example, *Tony is a walking encyclopedia* could be changed to *Tony is a walking **computer.*** Challenge students to see how many variations they can create for each metaphor without losing the meaning.

2. Have students help create a deck of simile and/or metaphor cards. Using 3" × 5" blank index cards, direct students to write a simile or metaphor on one side of each card and the explanation of the simile or metaphor on the opposite side. Have students use the cards to quiz each other about the meanings of the similes or metaphors.

# Activity 4—Ranking Meanings
## Form A

Name: _____  Date: _____

### Directions

Read each paragraph. Notice that a simile or a metaphor appears in bold letters in each paragraph. Use the scale provided to rank three possible meanings for each simile or metaphor relationship. Be prepared to discuss your answers. An example has been provided to get you started. Ask questions if you need assistance.

| **1** | **2** | **3** |
|:---:|:---:|:---:|
| **the best comparison** | **an OK comparison** | **the most unlikely comparison** |

### Example

The aging athlete moved slowly. He didn't know how much longer his body would hold up. He already had shoulder and knee surgery, and his shoulder was starting to bother him again. He didn't want to tell the team doctor about the pain, because he knew what the doctor would say. **But the thought of retirement was as distant as the stars.**

**Relationship:** thought of retirement ➞ distant stars

___*2*___ in heaven   ___*1*___ remote   ___*3*___ shiny

1. My grandmother always had these sayings or expressions, like **"Tomorrow is but a promise,** make the most of today." She liked to tell me that when I complained that I was bored and had nothing to do. I didn't exactly know what she meant, but I didn't want to ask. One day I figured it out. Tomorrow is not guaranteed; something could happen today and your life would be over. So now when she says, "Tomorrow is but a promise," I understand what she's really telling me.

   **Relationship:** tomorrow ➞ a promise

   ____ not a guarantee   ____ a vow or pledge   ____ a weekend

**Figurative Language** © 2002 Thinking Publications
Duplication permitted for educational use only.

**Figurative Language**

2. The jury had just returned and was about to give the verdict. The defendant was scared and nervous. He had never felt like this in his life. **His heart was pounding like a bass drum in a marching band.**

**Relationship:** heart pounding → bass drum

_____ battering _____ beating _____ instrument

3. Destiny loved her new home. She took great pride in decorating it and adding special touches like new paintings for the living room. She carefully shopped for each new piece of furniture to make sure it was just the right one. **Destiny's home was her security blanket.**

**Relationship:** home → security blanket

_____ feeling of comfort _____ a sure thing _____ expensive

4. Derrick was excited about getting his first car. He went out of his way to take extremely good care it. It was always washed and waxed. It never had a speck of dust on the inside, and the windows and mirrors sparkled in the sun. Derrick loved to hear it run. **The sound of the engine was softer than a lullaby.**

**Relationship:** engine → a lullaby

_____ loud _____ a soothing lull _____ steady and low

72

**Figurative Language** © 2002 Thinking Publications
Duplication permitted for educational use only.

*Chapter 2: Metaphors and Similes*

# Activity 4—Ranking Meanings
## Form B

Name: _____     Date: _____

### Directions

Read each paragraph. Notice that a simile or a metaphor appears in bold letters in each paragraph. Use the scale provided to rank three possible meanings for each simile or metaphor relationship. Be prepared to discuss your answers. An example has been provided to get you started. Ask questions if you need assistance.

| 1 | 2 | 3 |
|:---:|:---:|:---:|
| **the best comparison** | **an OK comparison** | **the most unlikely comparison** |

### Example

Each year, before the flowers bloomed, the winds came. The wind was so strong and powerful that it practically moved everything in its path. It made walking in it almost impossible. From inside, you could hear it roar as it raced through the valley. **The howling wind was a pack of hungry wolves.**

**Relationship:** howling wind → hungry wolves

___3___ nervous     ___1___ loud and unstoppable     ___2___ swift

1. It was hard to forget the sound of that terrible storm. The wind blew fiercely for what seemed like an eternity. In a matter of hours, the once peaceful paradise of South Florida was in ruin. When we finally emerged from what was left of our house, total destruction was as far as the eye could see. **The hurricane was a freight train smashing into a cement wall.**

   **Relationship:** hurricane → freight train

   _____ extremely noisy     _____ large and long     _____ a machine

**Figurative Language** © 2002 Thinking Publications
Duplication permitted for educational use only.

**Figurative Language**

2. The score was tied 7 to 7, and it was the bottom of the ninth inning. This was the seventh game in the series, and the winner of this game would be the new World Champion. The excitement increased with every play, and soon the bases were loaded. When the star hitter approached home plate, the noise in the stadium became deafening. With the crack of the bat, the ball soared over the center field wall. **The opposing team's hearts sank into a field of quicksand.**

**Relationship:** hearts ➞ quicksand

_____ heavy and sinking     _____ soft     _____ muddy

---

3. It was hard to believe that Graduation Day was finally here. Jamie had struggled each day just to get a passing grade. Many times he told himself that it was useless to try to get a high school diploma. His parents and teachers constantly reminded him that it was worth the effort to keep trying. Now he was standing in line, ready to receive his diploma. When his name was called, **Jamie's head was a balloon that carried him across the stage.**

**Relationship:** Jamie's head ➞ balloon

_____ empty     _____ feeling swollen     _____ plastic

---

4. The well-dressed man walked up to the lunch counter and waited to be served. There was nothing unusual about this except that this was Alabama in 1963, and the man was African American. He wasn't served lunch, but rather taken to jail for breaking the law. It took many years and many similar acts of civil disobedience before the laws changed. Today, the same well-dressed man sits in a restaurant with his grandchildren, waiting to be served. The waitress ignores him and serves a customer that was seated later. The man explains to his grandchildren, "Laws change, but **attitudes are stones that won't be moved.**"

**Relationship:** attitudes ➞ stones

_____ hard     _____ round     _____ unchanging

*Chapter 2: Metaphors and Similes*

# Activity 4—Ranking Meanings
## Answer Key

**Form A (pgs 71–72)**

1. tomorrow ➜ a promise
   1—not a guarantee
   2—a vow or pledge
   3—a weekend

2. heart pounding ➜ bass drum
   2—battering
   1—beating
   3—instrument

3. home ➜ security
   1—feeling of comfort
   2—a sure thing
   3—expensive

4. engine ➜ lullaby
   3—loud
   1—a soothing lull
   2—steady and low

**Form B (pgs 73–74)**

1. hurricane ➜ freight train
   1—extremely noisy
   2—large and long
   3—a machine

2. hearts ➜ quicksand
   1—heavy and sinking
   2—soft
   3—muddy

3. Jamie's head ➜ balloon
   2—empty
   1—feeling swollen
   3—plastic

4. attitudes ➜ stones
   2—hard
   3—round
   1—unchanging

75

**Figurative Language**

# Activity 4—Ranking Meanings
## Extension Ideas

1. Using the tasks provided in Activity 4, have students underline or highlight the words from the paragraphs that give clues to the meanings of the similes and metaphors. Then have students explain their responses.

2. Have students use a thesaurus to locate synonyms for the various characteristics that are presented in Activity 4. For instance, the example provided on Form A shows the most closely related characteristic between *dreams* and *distant stars* is that they are both remote. Students can find that *remote* has synonyms, such as *solitary, aloof, uncommunicative,* and *withdrawn.* Discuss with students whether the synonyms they locate make sense in place of the characteristics provided in the activity tasks.

# Idioms

## Chapter 3

## What Are Idioms?

Idioms are figures of speech that can have both literal and nonliteral interpretations. Idiomatic expressions change over time, and they are found in all languages and across all modes of communication (Ezell and Goldstein, 1992). Idioms include expressions such as *hit the roof, kick the bucket,* and *chew the fat.* By definition, an idiom is a construction or string of words for which the intended meaning in context is different from its literal meaning. The assignment of a new meaning to a phrase or sentence that already has its own meaning distinguishes idioms from other forms of figurative language (Boatner and Gates, 1975). Idioms are extremely diverse in their etymological, syntactic, semantic, and pragmatic properties (Nippold, 1991). When used frequently, an idiom becomes an accepted part of a language and the construction is considered frozen. Idioms appear frequently in conversations, lectures, movies, radio and television broadcasts, and newspapers (Nippold, 1991).

## Review of the Literature

Idioms are common in both spoken and written language. It has been estimated that two-thirds of the English language consists of idiomatic expressions (Arnold and Hornett, 1990; Boatner and Gates, 1975). At grade 3 (ages 8–9 years), an average of 6% of the sentences in students' literature contain at least one idiom, and by grade 8, that average increases to 10% (Nippold, Moran, and Schwarz, 2001).

Early developmental research indicated that idioms were processed somewhat differently than other forms of language. Lodge and Leach (1975) discussed the distinction between literal and nonliteral interpretations. Their work supported a stage theory in which the literal meaning is acquired

**Figurative Language**

first, followed by the nonliteral meaning. Subsequent research supported a more holistic view of processing, with idioms being understood as giant lexical units (Ackerman, 1982; Gibbs, 1986, 1991). While current researchers continue to investigate how idioms are processed and why some idioms are easier to interpret than others, most agree that context is an important part of investigating idiom interpretation, as well as teaching idioms in the classroom (Ackerman, 1982; Cacciari and Levorato, 1989; Gibbs, 1991; Nippold, 1991; Nippold, Moran, and Schwarz, 2001).

Some of these same researchers have found factors of idiom familiarity and transparency to influence idiom interpretation (Gibbs, 1991; Nippold, Moran, and Schwarz, 2001; Nippold and Taylor, 1995, 1996). Familiarity is a measure of how frequently one has heard or read an expression. Transparency is a measure of how closely the literal and nonliteral meanings of the expression compare (Nippold and Taylor, 1995; Nippold, Moran, and Schwarz, 2001). For example, in students' rating of familiarity, the idiom *skating on thin ice* was more familiar than was *paper over the cracks* (Nippold, Moran, and Schwarz, 2001). Likewise, in students' ratings of transparency, *go around in circles* was more transparent than *beat around the bush* (Nippold and Rudzinski, 1993).

Prior exposure to idioms appears to support the "language experience" view that the more exposure one has to idiomatic language, the better one will be able to interpret it (Nippold and Rudzinski, 1993; Ortony et al., 1985a, 1985b). However, mere exposure to idioms does not ensure that the same idiom presented later on will be understood (Nippold, 1991). Students deficient in reading and comprehension skills may not benefit from prior exposure to idioms and may need specific strategies to teach idiom interpretation (Ackerman, 1982; Levorato and Cacciari, 1992; Nippold, 1991; Nippold, Moran, and Schwarz, 2001). Speakers of languages other than English may have difficulty understanding English idioms and may benefit from specific instruction (Irujo, 1986; May, 1979). If poor comprehenders of idioms are not provided with special instruction, it is likely they will continue to lag behind their peers and the gap will continue to widen as they move through adolescence and into adulthood (Nippold, Moran, and Schwarz, 2001).

# Developmental Information

Children as young as age 5 appear to understand some nonliteral meanings of idioms. This understanding continues to increase throughout adolescence (Brinton, Fujiki, and Mackey, 1985; Douglas and Peel, 1979; Lodge and Leach, 1975; Nippold, Allen, and Kirsch, 2001). In addition, understanding of idioms precedes accurate use of such expressions. Development of nonliteral understanding and use of idiomatic expressions tends to parallel cognitive development (Lodge and Leach, 1975).

*Chapter 3: Idioms*

# How Can This Chapter Be Used?

There are five activities in Chapter 3. It is recommended that you begin with Activity 1, as the activities progress from easier to more challenging tasks. However, use discretion and feel free to pick and choose activities to meet the particular needs of each student. It is recommended that the card game described in Activity 5 be conducted after students have been exposed to the preceding activities within the chapter. Take time before each activity to discuss the difference between *literal* and *figurative,* and display these definitions for all to see to make completing the activities easier.

- **Activity 1** asks students to identify and label the literal versus the figurative interpretation of an idiom that appears in a short-story context. The contextual support of the story helps students accurately interpret the given idioms. Form A and Form B are provided for Activity 1, as is an answer key and extensions ideas.

- **Activity 2** also asks students to identify and label the literal versus the figurative interpretation of an idiom, but less contextual support is provided than in Activity 1. The given idioms appear in a single sentence rather than a short story. Activity 2 includes Form A and Form B, plus an answer key and extension ideas.

- **Activity 3** taps into understanding and use of idiomatic expressions. Students choose an idiom to complete a short story. Then students are asked to describe a situation they are familiar with that is similar to the one expressed in the given story. Form A and Form B are provided for Activity 3, as is an answer key and extension ideas.

- **Activity 4** presents illustrations that convey literal interpretations of idioms. Students are asked to overcome each literal meaning and use the figurative meaning for each idiom to write a situation in which the idiom would apply. Activity 4 includes Form A, Form B, and Form C, as well as extension ideas.

- **Activity 5** presents directions and a list of idioms for creating a card game to target students' understanding and use of these expressions. (Also consider using idioms from the classroom curriculum and from students' daily lives for this activity.)

For all five activities, encourage students to talk about the possible meanings of each idiom as the tasks are discussed and completed. Also, direct students to read the tasks aloud to help them better recognize whether their response is accurate. Demonstrate and encourage the use of context cues and reference materials (e.g., an idiom dictionary) to help students understand and use idioms. Refer to "Suggested Adaptations" (page 7) for optional reading and writing adaptations.

Perhaps not enough can be said about the importance of context, which is especially true when teaching correct idiom interpretation. A supportive context will lead the learner to the correct nonliteral

83

**Figurative Language**

interpretation. However, context that is ambiguous may lead to confusion and inaccurate interpretations. The contexts provided in this chapter are designed for either the literal or nonliteral interpretation of an idiom, so that only one correct answer is possible. The targeted idiom appears in bold type, so that it stands out from the rest of the context. Direct instruction of literal and nonliteral interpretations is necessary, so that students can understand and complete the idiom activities in this chapter. Students who can distinguish between the literal and nonliteral forms will be able to complete the activities in this chapter with greater ease.

Consider the activity pages as discussion guides rather than as paper-and-pencil tasks. Bridge discussions by talking about when students might encounter the given idioms in their academic and/or personal lives.

*Chapter 3: Idioms*

# Activity 1—Identifying Literal and Figurative Meanings of Idioms in Stories
## Form A

Name: _____     Date: _____

### Directions

Idioms are expressions that have two meanings—a literal meaning and a figurative meaning. Read each paragraph below. For each phrase in bold, choose the best meaning by circling either *a* or *b*. Then write an *F* or an *L* in the box to indicate whether the phrase is being used in a **Figurative** or a **Literal** way in the given paragraph. Be prepared to discuss your answers. Ask questions if you need assistance.

1. Jade was already angry with her sister for borrowing her favorite sweater and losing it. Now her sister was also using her makeup without asking. Her sister was just **adding fuel to the fire.**

   a. Jade's sister was pouring gasoline on a campfire.

   b. Jade's sister was making a bad situation worse.

2. Shakira and her friends were talking about the latest talk shows that feature family problems and Court TV shows that publicize the silliest lawsuits imaginable. Disgusted, Shakira said, "I am sick of people who **air their dirty laundry in public!"**

   a. Shakira thinks people should not broadcast their personal, private problems in a public way.

   b. Shakira thinks people should hang only clean clothes outside to dry.

**Figurative Language** © 2002 Thinking Publications
Duplication permitted for educational use only.

85

**Figurative Language**

☐ 3. Kareem was looking forward to the annual family reunion picnic. Because so many people came, there weren't enough chairs, so Kareem ended up sitting on the ground to eat. Unfortunately, he sat on an ant hill and got **ants in his pants.**

    a. Kareem had insects in his pants.

    b. Kareem drank too much soda and couldn't sit still at the picnic.

☐ 4. Sarah had a car and often drove her friends to school. She was a good driver and didn't want anyone to tell her how to drive. She often told her friends, "I'll give you a ride, but I don't want anyone to be a **backseat driver."**

    a. Sarah didn't want anyone to tell her how to drive.

    b. Sarah's car had a steering wheel in the backseat that she didn't want used.

☐ 5. Anika was always tired. She was a single mother and worked two jobs. One of her jobs was 25 miles away from home. The day she had an accident, she was **asleep at the wheel.**

    a. Anika wasn't doing her job correctly and was fired.

    b. Because she was drowsy, Anika fell asleep while she was driving and had an accident.

☐ 6. Hillary was excited about her new, customized computer. It was everything she wanted: a CD burner, a scanner, a digital web cam, and a laser printer. I said to her, "It certainly has **all the bells and whistles,** doesn't it?"

    a. Hillary's computer sounds like a train.

    b. Hillary's computer has all the latest technology.

**Figurative Language** © 2002 Thinking Publications
Duplication permitted for educational use only.

*Chapter 3: Idioms*

☐ 7. Everyone in Judy's family went to college and got into successful careers, except for Judy. Judy dropped out of high school and ended up in jail. Judy seem to be the **black sheep of the family.**

    a. Judy got a job on a farm raising sheep.

    b. Judy was quite different from the rest of her family.

☐ 8. Our class went on a hayride last week. It was a lot of fun, but a few students got out of hand. They were throwing hay at each other, and it caused one of the students to **fall off the wagon.**

    a. The student fell from the hay wagon.

    b. The student was drinking alcohol again.

☐ 9. Sasha knew she might be receiving a failing grade in her math class. The day before report cards were to be handed out, Sasha told her math teacher that she liked her hairdo and outfit. Sasha thought, "That should **butter her up.**"

    a. Sasha thought it would make the teacher feel flattered.

    b. Sasha spread butter on the teacher.

☐ 10. Ramon sneaks tastes of his mother's cooking before it is done. Ramon denies it whenever his mother asks if he's the one sneaking tastes. One day, Ramon's mom walked into the kitchen and **caught him red-handed** as Ramon was putting food into his mouth.

    a. Ramon's hands were red.

    b. Ramon was caught in the act of sneaking a taste of his mother's food.

**Figurative Language** © 2002 Thinking Publications
Duplication permitted for educational use only.

**Figurative Language**

# Activity 1—Identifying Literal and Figurative Meanings of Idioms in Stories
## Form B

Name: _____  Date: _____

## Directions

Idioms are expressions that have two meanings—a literal meaning and a figurative meaning. Read each paragraph below. For each phrase in bold, choose the best meaning by circling either *a* or *b*. Then write an *F* or an *L* in the box to indicate whether the phrase is being used in a **Figurative** or a **Literal** way in the given paragraph. Be prepared to discuss your answers. Ask questions if you need assistance.

☐ 1. Shannon bought a new designer purse at the flea market. She was excited about the great deal she got on such an expensive item. Shannon became upset when her purse started to **come apart at the seams.**

    a. Shannon couldn't control her excitement about her new purse.

    b. Shannon's designer purse started to fall apart.

☐ 2. I just subscribed to a new magazine called *Techno Wiz.* It has all the latest information on computers and high-tech gadgets. Some people think it's mostly science fiction, but I think it's on the **cutting edge.**

    a. The magazine has current information.

    b. The magazine should be cut up.

**Figurative Language** © 2002 Thinking Publications
Duplication permitted for educational use only.

88

*Chapter 3: Idioms*

3. My mom is always doing home-improvement projects. She is pretty good, but once in a while she makes a mistake. Recently, when she was putting up a ceiling fan, she put a hole in the ceiling. Her hammer slipped and she **hit the roof.**

   a. She put a hole in the roof with a hammer.

   b. She got angry because of her mistake.

4. Janice's mom needed to run a few errands, so she asked Janice to watch her younger sister and brother until she got back. Janice said, "Sure Mom, I'll **hold down the fort.**"

   a. Janice would take care of the house and children in her mother's absence.

   b. Janice would take the children to a fort.

5. Brittany has an extensive stuffed-animal collection. She thinks that her dolls are rare and worth a lot of money. The stuffed animals are not very original, and I think they are **a dime a dozen.**

   a. I think Brittany's animal collection is worth 10 cents.

   b. I think Brittany's animal collection isn't rare.

6. Erica grilled some sirloin steaks for dinner. She warned us they were an inexpensive cut of meat and said, "Be careful not to **chew the fat.**"

   a. Erica warned us not to have a long conversation.

   b. Erica did not want us to choke on the fat of the meat.

**Figurative Language** © 2002 Thinking Publications
Duplication permitted for educational use only.

**Figurative Language**

☐ 7. Daniel was tired of all the rumors about his friend being a thief and a drug dealer. He knew they weren't true. Daniel said, "I'm **going to bat** for you."

   a. Daniel was going to support his friend.

   b. Daniel wanted to play baseball on his friend's team.


☐ 8. Shelly couldn't concentrate at all. She always seemed to be distracted and confused. Her friends often thought that she was **out to lunch** when they tried to talk to her.

   a. Her friends thought Shelly had a date for lunch.

   b. Her friends thought Shelly was not alert.


☐ 9. Jared was always getting scolded by the teacher. First it was for talking, then it was for pushing another student, and then it was because he was **out of line** as the class walked outside for recess.

   a. Jared was unrealistic.

   b. Jared wasn't standing in line properly.


☐ 10. Christian liked to play with matches. He was fascinated with seeing things burn. No matter how many times he was told, he couldn't stop **playing with fire.**

   a. Christian used fire as if it were at toy.

   b. Christian took a big risk.

*Figurative Language* © 2002 Thinking Publications
Duplication permitted for educational use only.

90

*Chapter 3: Idioms*

# Activity 1—Identifying Literal and Figurative Meanings of Idioms in Stories
## Answer Key

**Form A (pgs 85–87)**

1. F, b
2. F, a
3. L, a
4. F, a
5. L, b
6. F, b
7. F, b
8. L, a
9. F, a
10. F, b

**Form B (pgs 88–90)**

1. L, b
2. F, a
3. L, a
4. F, a
5. F, b
6. L, b
7. F, a
8. F, b
9. L, b
10. L, a

Figurative Language

# Activity 1—Identifying Literal and Figurative Meanings of Idioms in Stories
## Extension Ideas

1. Have students underline or highlight words in the paragraphs in Activity 1 that gave them clues to the meaning of each idiom. Have students explain their responses.

2. Have students illustrate the figurative meaning of one or more of the idioms in Activity 1. Encourage students to use magazine pictures, their own drawings, and/or computerized graphics to create their illustrations. Have students share their illustrations when completed.

*Chapter 3: Idioms*

# Activity 2—Identifying Literal and Figurative Meanings of Idioms in Sentences
## Form A

Name: _____ Date: _____

### Directions

Each sentence below uses an idiom in a figurative way. Read each sentence and the two interpretations that follow each. Label one interpretation with an **F** if it explains the **F**igurative meaning of the idiom in bold. Label the other interpretation with an **L** if it explains the **L**iteral meaning. Be prepared to discuss your answers. Ask questions if you need assistance.

**1** We need some **new blood** on this team if we ever hope to win.

_____ a new team member

_____ a pint of blood

**2** **Cut corners** making this quilt by using material from some old shirts.

_____ economize to save money

_____ cut the corners off of the quilt

**3** He had to lift weights and **beef up** to enter the Mr. Universe contest.

_____ cook with meat

_____ add muscle and weight to get in shape

**4** We had to **iron out** our differences before we signed the contract.

_____ press our clothes

_____ agree on the details

**Figurative Language** © 2002 Thinking Publications
Duplication permitted for educational use only.

93

**Figurative Language**

**5** We all had to **chip in** for the surprise party for our boss.

_____ help pay for something

_____ put a crack in something

**6** I told my workers to stop the **monkey business** and get back to work, or they'd be fired.

_____ selling monkeys

_____ fooling around, not working seriously

**7** Living in New York City can be such a **rat race.**

_____ a frustrating, hectic experience

_____ a race between rodents

**8** I like coaching this team, but I have to work hard to keep these fellas **in line.**

_____ keep the players in a straight line

_____ have the players behave and follow the rules

**9** I'll be leaving the office in a few minutes. I have to take care of some **loose ends.**

_____ take care of some final details

_____ tie some ribbons together

**10** I'm tired of the **sob story** you keep giving me about your homework.

_____ crying while reading a story

_____ trying to get sympathy for a problem

*Chapter 3: Idioms*

# Activity 2—Identifying Literal and Figurative Meanings of Idioms in Sentences
## Form B

Name: _____     Date: _____

### Directions

Each sentence below uses an idiom in a figurative way. Read each sentence and the two interpretations that follow each. Label one interpretation with an *F* if it explains the **F**igurative meaning of the idiom in bold. Label the other interpretation with an *L* if it explains the **L**iteral meaning. Be prepared to discuss your answers. Ask questions if you need assistance.

**1**  I had to **pull some strings** to get these concert tickets.

_____ pull on some ropes

_____ use friendship to get a favor


**2**  I came to **talk turkey,** not to socialize.

_____ talk about turkeys

_____ talk about business


**3**  I'd like to give my **two cents** and tell you what my ideas are.

_____ pay two pennies

_____ tell my ideas, my point of view


**4**  I am really going to **shake up** this place when I show up in this outfit.

_____ shock or surprise people

_____ make a milk shake


**Figurative Language** © 2002 Thinking Publications
Duplication permitted for educational use only.

95

**Figurative Language**

**5** I need to **make tracks** to the store before the 4-hour sale ends.

_____ move quickly

_____ make tracks in the mud with my car

**6** Building the house is **in limbo** until we get the money to finish it.

_____ in the middle of a dance

_____ in an unfinished or indefinite state

**7** Don't get her started talking about her dog; she will **rattle on** for hours.

_____ shake an object

_____ talk too much

**8** The extent of the disaster didn't **sink in** until I realized I could not return home.

_____ become meaningful

_____ become submerged in water

**9** If John was going to run in the marathon, he was going to have to **shape up.**

_____ to become physically fit

_____ to form or make something

**10** After a long day at the office, Glenn was ready to **sack out.**

_____ get out a bag

_____ go to sleep

**Figurative Language** © 2002 Thinking Publications
Duplication permitted for educational use only.

*Chapter 3: Idioms*

# Activity 2—Identifying Literal and Figurative Meanings of Idioms in Sentences
## Answer Key

**Form A (pgs 93–94)**
1. F, L
2. F, L
3. L, F
4. L, F
5. F, L
6. L, F
7. F, L
8. L, F
9. F, L
10. L, F

**Form B (pgs 95–96)**
1. L, F
2. L, F
3. L, F
4. F, L
5. F, L
6. L, F
7. L, F
8. F, L
9. F, L
10. L, F

**Figurative Language**

# Activity 2—Identifying Literal and Figurative Meanings of Idioms in Sentences

## Extension Ideas

1. Have students tell or write about idiom examples of their own. Encourage students to collect and bring in examples of idioms they encounter throughout their daily lives. Have students describe the context in which the idiom occurred and both the figurative and the literal interpretations of the idiom.

2. Have students keep track of idioms using blank 3" × 5" index cards. As idioms are discussed in class, have a student write the idiom in the context of a sentence on one side of an index card and write the figurative and literal interpretations of the idiom on the other side of the card. Keep a running file of these idiom cards. Consider awarding students bonus points for bringing completed cards to class.

*Chapter 3: Idioms*

# Activity 3—Choosing and Using Idioms
## Form A

Name: _____     Date: _____

### Directions

Choose the idiom that best completes each of the following stories. Place an *X* in the blank next to your choice. Then describe a situation that is similar to the one provided. Be prepared to discuss your answers. Ask questions if you need assistance.

**1** When I was talking to my friend on the telephone, I forgot the name of the restaurant my family had eaten at last weekend. It was my favorite place to eat. I know I'll think of it soon because it's…

_____ a shot in the dark
_____ on the tip of my tongue
_____ a chip off the old block

Give an example of a similar situation: _____

_____

_____

**2** Tanya was being unrealistic. She thought that she could just walk into the hardware store and smile and the store owner would donate money and materials for her class dance. She wouldn't listen to us, so we told her to go ahead and try. After no success, she had to…

_____ cry over spilled milk
_____ do a double take
_____ come down to Earth

Give an example of a similar situation: _____

_____

_____

**Figurative Language** © 2002 Thinking Publications
Duplication permitted for educational use only.

**Figurative Language**

**3** Shane has the most beat-up car I have ever seen. I don't know how he even gets it started in the morning. The brakes are so squeaky that you can hear them two blocks away. Shane's car is…

_____ on the up and up

_____ an accident waiting to happen

_____ on easy street

Give an example of a similar situation: _____

_____

_____

**4** Bill started to mention the unpleasant and controversial topic of gun control. Not wanting a lengthy debate to get started, Bill's good friend said to him, "Please don't start with that topic. You'll just…

_____ open a can of worms

_____ lie through your teeth

_____ beat around the bush

Give an example of a similar situation: _____

_____

_____

**5** The new movie was supposed to be good. However, I was offended by the profanity, and the jokes were…

_____ in poor taste

_____ in the pink

_____ in the thick of it

Give an example of a similar situation: _____

_____

_____

**Figurative Language** © 2002 Thinking Publications
Duplication permitted for educational use only.

*Chapter 3: Idioms*

# Activity 3—Choosing and Using Idioms
## Form B

Name: _____    Date: _____

### Directions

Choose the idiom that best completes each of the following stories. Place an *X* in the blank next to your choice. Then describe a situation that is similar to the one provided. Be prepared to discuss your answers. Ask questions if you need assistance.

**1**  Juan knew that the car looked really bad, but he hoped that his parents would let him explain what happened before they:

_____ came up empty handed

_____ jumped to conclusions

_____ upset the apple cart

Give an example of a similar situation: _____

_____

_____

**2**  The candidate for mayor liked to talk. He had a bad habit of going off the subject and making long-winded speeches. The sponsor of the benefit warned the candidate to keep his speech…

_____ in the thick of it

_____ on the level

_____ short and sweet

Give an example of a similar situation: _____

_____

_____

**Figurative Language** © 2002 Thinking Publications
Duplication permitted for educational use only.

101

**Figurative Language**

**3**

He may be the president of the company, but he has others to help him make the tough decisions. In reality, it's his secretary that is the...

_____ power behind the throne

_____ real McCoy

_____ power and the fury

Give an example of a similar situation: _____

_____

_____


**4**

Jeremy was investing in the stock market for the first time. He wanted to put all of his money into a new company because the stocks were a bargain at the moment. His wife warned him not to...

_____ put all his eggs in one basket

_____ change horses midstream

_____ weasel out of it

Give an example of a similar situation: _____

_____

_____


**5**

Terrance was having a great time at the party, but it was getting late. He had to work in the morning. Some of his friends wanted to go out for some coffee, but Terrance decided to...

_____ take a break

_____ take a rain check

_____ take it for granted

Give an example of a similar situation: _____

_____

_____

**Figurative Language** © 2002 Thinking Publications
Duplication permitted for educational use only.

102

*Chapter 3: Idioms*

# Activity 3—Choosing and Using Idioms
## Answer Key

**Form A (pgs 99–100)**
1. on the tip of my tongue
2. come down to Earth
3. an accident waiting to happen
4. open a can of worms
5. in poor taste

**Form B (pgs 101–102)**
1. jumped to conclusions
2. short and sweet
3. power behind the throne
4. put all his eggs in one basket
5. take a rain check

**Figurative Language**

# Activity 3—
# Choosing and Using Idioms
## Extension Ideas

1. Have students illustrate or locate the intended meanings of the idioms presented in the Activity 3 pages. For example, a student might draw a picture of a stack of boxes that is so high it is about to topple over in order to illustrate the idiomatic expression *an accident waiting to happen.*

2. Have students locate and bring in examples of idioms they encounter in popular media (e.g., radio, magazines, and TV). For example, a student might bring in a magazine advertisement for a weight-reduction pill that asks, "What have you got to lose?"

*Chapter 3: Idioms*

# Activity 4—
# Understanding and Applying Idioms
## Form A

Name: _____  Date: _____

**Directions**

Sometimes the literal meaning of an idiom can be shown in a drawing, but the drawing does not help explain or show the figurative meaning of the idiom. The following pictures show the literal meanings of each idiom. Read the explanation of the figurative meaning of each idiom, and then suggest an example that goes along with the meaning. Be prepared to discuss your answers. Ask questions if you need assistance.

1. **Bend over backward.**

*Bend over backward* means:

- Try to help someone  OR
- Do more than most to help someone out of a difficult situation

Give an example of a situation that would go with this idiom: _____

_____

_____

Figurative Language © 2002 Thinking Publications
Duplication permitted for educational use only.

Figurative Language

2. **Get a foot in the door.**

*Get a foot in the door* means:
- Get a first chance, or opportunity to do something   OR
- Get a career opportunity

Give an example of a situation that would go with this idiom: _____
_____
_____

3. **Hold your tongue.**

*Hold your tongue* means:
- Do not say anything when you really want to say something   OR
- Show restraint when you want to make your knowledge or opinion known

Give an example of a situation that would go with this idiom: _____
_____
_____

*Figurative Language* © 2002 Thinking Publications
Duplication permitted for educational use only.

*Chapter 3: Idioms*

# Activity 4—
# Understanding and Applying Idioms
## Form B

Name: _____   Date: _____

**Directions**

Sometimes the literal meaning of an idiom can be shown in a drawing, but the drawing does not help explain or show the figurative meaning of the idiom. The following pictures show the literal meanings of each idiom. Read the explanation of the figurative meaning of each idiom, and then suggest an example that goes along with the meaning. Be prepared to discuss your answers. Ask questions if you need assistance.

1. **Put your best foot forward.**

*Put your best foot forward* means:

- Show off your positive traits   OR
- Attempt to impress others or make a positive impression

Give an example of a situation that would go with this idiom: _____

_____

_____

*Figurative Language* © 2002 Thinking Publications
Duplication permitted for educational use only.

107

Figurative Language

2. **Sharp tongued.**

*Sharp tongued* means:
- Saying unkind things to or about someone   OR
- Being critical about what other people do

Give an example of a situation that would go with this idiom: _____
_____
_____

3. **Put your foot in your mouth.**

*Put your foot in your mouth* means:
- Said something foolish or offensive   OR
- Said something you instantly regretted saying

Give an example of a situation that would go with this idiom: _____
_____
_____

*Chapter 3: Idioms*

# Activity 4—
# Understanding and Applying Idioms
## Form C

Name: _____   Date: _____

**Directions**

Sometimes the literal meaning of an idiom can be shown in a drawing, but the drawing does not help explain or show the figurative meaning of the idiom. The following pictures show the literal meanings of each idiom. Read the explanation of the figurative meaning of each idiom, and then suggest an example that goes along with the meaning. Be prepared to discuss your answers. Ask questions if you need assistance.

1. **Take the bull by the horns.**

*Take the bull by the horns* means:

- Act bravely in a difficult situation   OR
- Become active in times of trouble

Give an example of a situation that would go with this idiom: _____

_____

_____

**Figurative Language** © 2002 Thinking Publications
Duplication permitted for educational use only.

109

Figurative Language

2. **Throw in the towel.**

**Throw in the towel** means:
- Give up or quit   OR
- Stop trying or making efforts toward a cause

Give an example of a situation that would go with this idiom: _____
_____
_____

3. **Up a creek without a paddle.**

*Up a creek without a paddle* means:
- Have few or no alternatives to solve a problem
- Be in serious trouble without a realistic way to help yourself out

Give an example of a situation that would go with this idiom: _____
_____
_____

# Activity 4—Understanding and Applying Idioms
## Extension Ideas

1. For an activity that adds extra challenge, have students draw pictures that represent the figurative interpretations of selected idioms (e.g., drawing a picture of a person lifting weights while eating to represent the expression *beef up*). Some idioms whose figurative meanings are easier to depict include

   - *beef up*
   - *snowed in*
   - *caught red-handed*
   - *copy cat*
   - *eat like a bird*
   - *hit the roof*
   - *out of breath*

   - *pay an arm and a leg*
   - *playing with fire*
   - *hit the books*
   - *button your lip*
   - *sitting pretty*
   - *bring home the bacon*
   - *have eyes bigger than one's stomach*

2. As idioms appear in classroom discussions, have students explain why the literal interpretation of an idiom is not the true intent of the message.

**Figurative Language**

# Activity 4—Idioms Card Game

## Directions

Create an idioms card deck. Choose from the examples provided below, or use idioms from students' classroom curriculum and daily lives. For each example, write the idiom on one side of a 3" × 5" index card and the figurative meaning on the other side of the card. If possible, have students help create the card deck.

Group students into two teams. Place the deck in the center of a table with the meanings facedown. Have teams take turns choosing the top card from the deck and saying the idiom aloud to the other team. The responding team must then state the figurative meaning of the given idiom. If the responding team is successful, they keep the card. If the responding team is not successful, the card should be returned to the bottom of the deck. The team with the most cards at the end wins.

NOTE: Alternate options include the following:

- Write the idioms on one set of cards and the figurative meanings on another set of cards. Then use the two decks to play a classic game of Memory by having students match the idioms to their meanings.

- Have students group the various idioms according to categories, as suggested below. Encourage students to work together to sort the idioms. (Variation adapted from Nippold, 1991.)

| Idiom | Figurative Meaning | Category |
|---|---|---|
| adding fuel to the fire | making a bad situation worse | tools |
| air their dirty laundry in public | talk about personal problems in public | clothing |
| ants in his pants | act nervous and jittery | animals |
| backseat driver | telling the driver what to do | vehicles |
| asleep at the wheel | not paying attention | vehicles |
| all the bells and whistles | the latest luxury features | tools |
| black sheep of the family | different than other family members | animals |

*Chapter 3: Idioms*

| Idiom | Figurative Meaning | Category |
|---|---|---|
| fall off the wagon | start drinking after being sober | vehicles |
| butter her up | show flattery to get a favor | food |
| caught him red-handed | caught him doing something wrong | body parts |
| come apart at the seams | become unable to handle a difficult situation | clothing |
| cutting edge | to be the first to have the latest technology | tools |
| hit the roof | get angry | actions |
| hold down the fort | to be in charge | locations |
| a dime a dozen | very common, not rare | money |
| chew the fat | talk a while with someone | food |
| going to bat | giving support | actions |
| out to lunch | confused or unaware | food |
| out of line | to be unreasonable or uncontrolled | actions |
| playing with fire | acting dangerously | actions |
| new blood | a new member | body parts |
| cut corners | economize to save money or materials | tools |
| beef up | add muscle or weight to a body | food |
| iron out | organize or finalize details | tools |
| chip in | put money toward | actions |
| monkey business | fooling around and not being serious | animals |
| rat race | a hectic, competitive situation | animals |
| in line | well-behaved or reasonable | actions |
| loose ends | final details | tools |
| sob story | complaint to get sympathy for a problem | actions |
| pull some strings | use a relationship to get a favor | tools |
| talk turkey | discuss business | animals |
| two cents | an opinion or advice | money |
| shake up | shock or surprise others | actions |
| make tracks | move quickly | vehicles |
| in limbo | in a state of uncertainty | actions |
| rattle on | talk continuously | actions |
| sink in | understand or comprehend | actions |
| shape up | improve or start to behave | actions |

113

**Figurative Language**

| Idiom | Figurative Meaning | Category |
|---|---|---|
| sack out | fall asleep | actions |
| on the tip of my tongue | almost able to recall a detail | body parts |
| come down to Earth | become realistic or sensible | locations |
| an accident waiting to happen | something unsafe or unreliable | actions |
| open a can of worms | bring up a controversial topic | animals |
| in poor taste | offensive or rude | body parts |
| jumped to conclusions | make a hasty decision | actions |
| short and sweet | brief and concise | food |
| power behind the throne | the one actually in charge | locations |
| put all his eggs in one basket | put all his faith or money into one thing | food |
| take a rain check | ask to do something at a later time | money |
| bend over backward | go out of your way to help someone | actions |
| get a foot in the door | get a first chance or opportunity | body parts |
| hold your tongue | keep from saying something | body parts |
| put your best foot forward | show your positive traits | body parts |
| sharp tongued | says mean or negative things | body parts |
| put your foot in your mouth | say something foolish or regrettable | body parts |
| take the bull by the horns | act bravely in difficult times | animals |
| throw in the towel | give up | clothing |
| up a creek without a paddle | in serious trouble | tools |

# Proverbs

## Chapter 4

# What Are Proverbs?

Proverbs are colorful statements that are used to convey a general truth or wisdom, especially of a moral nature. According to Nippold (1985), proverbs are accepted phrases used to warn (e.g., *Waste not want not),* to advise (e.g., *Run after two hares and you will catch neither),* to encourage (e.g., *Every cloud has a silver lining),* or to comment (e.g., *All that glitters is not gold).* Sometimes proverbs even rhyme, as in Benjamin Franklin's *Early to bed, early to rise, makes a man healthy, wealthy, and wise.* Proverbs appear in almost every language, and every culture has its own unique forms of proverbial expressions. Proverbs appear in Greek mythology and religious writings. In the African American culture, a rhetoric style frequently used in preaching includes the use of proverbs (Ortony et al., 1985a, 1985b).

Proverbs are similar to idioms because they can have both literal and figurative interpretations. However, proverbs offer intriguing messages that require novel thinking about life (Nippold, Allen, and Kirsch, 2001). Watts (1950) explained that a proverb may be regarded as a fable condensed into a simple sentence. In fact, some of the more well-known proverbs are embedded in fables. A fable is a brief tale in which animals or inanimate objects speak and behave like humans. Aesop's Fables are among the best known fables and appear in many different languages. Aesop was supposed to have lived in the sixth century, BC, and never actually wrote down any of his fables. These stories have been told and retold until they were finally recorded in the first century, AD, in Latin and Greek. Because of their wide availability (e.g., *http://www.AesopFables.com* and *http://www.Zeus-publications.com/aesops.html*) and useful contexts, adapted versions of these famous fables appear in the activities in this chapter.

# Review of the Literature

Honeck, Sowry, and Voegtle (1978) questioned the validity of examining proverb comprehension in children by using explanation tasks. The problem with using an explanation task to measure children's proverb comprehension is that it may underestimate the child's true comprehension (Nippold, 1985; Nippold and Haq, 1996). Other problems with early investigations of proverb knowledge were with multiple-choice tasks that included literal and figurative interpretations (Gorham, 1956; Watts, 1950). These types of tasks did not specify that figurative interpretations were expected from the children. Current researchers avoid using proverbs in isolation, out of context, and with explanation demands for young children (Nippold, 1985; Nippold and Haq, 1996) when proverb comprehension is being measured. Instead, a top-down and bottom-up process is used. Recent studies (Nippold and Haq, 1996; Nippold et al., 2000; Nippold, Allen, and Kirsch, 2001) focus on context (i.e., a top-down concept), as well as word knowledge, concreteness, and familiarity (i.e., bottom-up factors). Results from this more recent research support the metasemantic hypothesis that proverbs are learned through a process of analyzing the individual word meanings in the proverb.

# Developmental Information

Early studies of proverb comprehension found that children have difficulty understanding this figurative form before adolescence (Billow, 1975; Douglas and Peel, 1979; Gorham, 1956; Richardson and Church, 1959; Watts, 1950). Proverbs, in comparison with metaphors and idioms, are considered more difficult for children to comprehend (Billow, 1975; Douglas and Peel, 1979). Concrete and familiar proverbs such as *The early bird catches the worm* are easier to comprehend than abstract and unfamiliar proverbs such as *A wonder lasts but nine days* (Nippold and Haq, 1996). As children progress through adolescence and into adulthood, their explanations of proverbs become more figurative (Billow, 1975; Douglas and Peel, 1979; Gorham, 1956; Richardson and Church, 1959; Watts, 1950). Furthermore, proverb explanation continues to increase throughout adolescence and adulthood (Nippold et al., 1997).

Although word knowledge is an important part of proverb comprehension, that knowledge alone does not ensure proverb comprehension; other factors appear to be involved. Nippold et al. (2000) provide the example *Two captains will sink a ship* as a concrete proverb that was understood by children 55% of the time. Yet, the corresponding nouns, *captain* and *ship* were understood with 100% accuracy. The other factors may include age, education, and world experience (Nippold, 1985; Nippold and Haq, 1996; Nippold et al., 2000; Nippold, Allen, and Kirsch, 2001).

# How Can This Chapter Be Used?

There are five activities in Chapter 4. Beginning with Activity 1 is recommended since the subsequent activities require more explanation and are increasingly challenging. However, feel free modify the order of certain activities to meet individual student needs. It is recommended that the card game described in Activity 5 be conducted after students have been exposed to the preceding activities within the chapter. Take time before each activity to discuss the difference between *literal* and *figurative* and display these definitions with samples for all to see to make completing the activities easier. Also acquaint students with the meanings of the words *fable* and *proverb* as the first activity is introduced.

- **Activity 1** requires students to demonstrate their understanding of proverbs embedded in familiar fables using a multiple-choice format. Forms A, B, and C are provided for Activity 1, as is an answer key and extension ideas.

- **Activity 2** requires students to recognize the main idea of a short story by choosing one of three proverbs that best matches the meaning of the story. Students are then asked to provide their own example situation related to the proverb. Three forms—A, B, and C—are provided for this activity, along with an answer key and extension ideas.

- **Activity 3** challenges students to recognize the virtue or ideal highlighted in familiar proverbs. Forms A, B, and C are provided for Activity 3, as well as an answer key and extension ideas.

- **Activity 4** presents short stories that contain proverbs and asks students to explain the meaning of each proverb. This activity includes Form A, Form B, and extension ideas.

- **Activity 5** presents directions and a list of proverbs for creating a card game to target students' understanding and use of these expressions.

For all five activities, encourage students to talk about the possible meanings of each proverb as the tasks are discussed and completed. Also, direct students to read the tasks aloud to help them better recognize whether their response is accurate. Refer to "Suggested Adaptations" (page 7) for optional reading and writing adaptations.

Consider the activity pages as discussion guides rather than as paper-and-pencil tasks. Bridge discussions by talking about when students might encounter proverbs in their academic and/or personal lives.

Understanding and interpreting proverbs is closely related to the contexts in which they are presented (Nippold, 1985). If the context changes, so does the meaning of the proverb. For example, *Rome was not built in a day* can have a literal interpretation: "It took a number of years to create the city of Rome" and a figurative interpretation: "It takes time to make great things." So, the intended meaning of this expression is solely dependent on the extended context within which it is used.

**Figurative Language**

As with other forms of figurative language, a supportive, biased context will facilitate proverb comprehension. Fables are typically the contextual support for the interpretation of proverbs and are often supportive and biased for proverb comprehension. Some proverbs that appear in isolation may contradict each other. For example *Too many cooks spoil the broth* and *Many hands make light work* seem to convey opposing messages. A supportive context for each of these proverbs would easily resolve this confusion (Hirsch, Kett, Trefil, 1988; Nippold, 1998). Help students understand how to use context cues in order to figure out the meanings of proverbs.

A context that is biased toward the figurative interpretation of a proverb is critical. Many of these contexts are available on the Internet. Use keywords such as *Aesop, fables,* and *proverbs* when searching for additional proverb contexts (e.g., fables) for targeting this linguistic structure. Nippold (1998) also provides an extensive list of proverbs, rated on their familiarity to adolescents and adults (p. 134–136 in her text).

*Chapter 4: Proverbs*

# Activity 1—
# Understanding Proverbs Used in Fables
## Form A

Name: _____    Date: _____

**Directions**

Fables are short stories that teach a lesson. The lesson in a fable is usually summarized in a statement called a *proverb*. A proverb is a single sentence that teaches a lesson or shows an example. Read and discuss the following fables. Notice that each fable ends with a proverb (shown in bold letters). Circle the letter of the best meaning for each proverb from the three choices provided. Be prepared to discuss your answers. Ask questions if you need assistance.

1. Once a father had a family of big, strong sons. One day, the father brought a tightly wrapped bundle of sticks and a hammer to his sons and said, "Go ahead and try to break the bundle." Each son took a turn to try to break the bundle, but no one could even break one stick. The father then opened the bundle and had his sons hit the sticks with a hammer. Each stick that was hit by itself broke. The father said, "I guess it's true of sticks too: **United we stand, divided we fall.**"

    *United we stand, divided we fall* means:
    a. If you work together, you will have a stronger defense than working alone.
    b. Sticks are strong, but only when tied up.
    c. Sticks and stones will break your bones.

**Figurative Language**

2. Once there was a hunter who came upon a small deer that he was about to kill. The deer pleaded, "Oh, please, spare me, and I will repay your kindness someday." The hunter laughed, "How could a pathetic creature like you ever help me?" The hunter added, "I'll let you go this time, but leave now before I change my mind." Soon afterward, a band of thieves came upon the hunter and left him tied to a tree in the woods. The small deer found the hunter and freed him by gnawing through the rope. The deer said, "You thought you would never need help, but **no man is an island.**"

   *No man is an island* means:

   a. We all need help from others from time to time.

   b. Men cannot live on an island very long.

   c. It's hard to say you're sorry.

3. An ant went to the bank of a river to quench its thirst. It got carried away by the rush of the stream and was about to drown. A dove sitting on a tree branch overhanging the water plucked a leaf and let it fall into the stream close to the ant. The ant climbed onto it and floated safely to the bank. Shortly afterward, a bird catcher came along and stood under the tree. He laid his net for the dove, which sat in the branches. The ant, seeing what the bird catcher was doing, stung him in the foot. In pain, the bird catcher threw down the net, and the noise made the dove fly away. It just goes to show that **one good turn deserves another.**

   *One good turn deserves another* means:

   a. Taking turns is important in friendship.

   b. Help someone else, and one day you, too, will be helped.

   c. Help is never around when you need it the most.

**Figurative Language** © 2002 Thinking Publications
Duplication permitted for educational use only.

120

*Chapter 4: Proverbs*

# Activity 1—
# Understanding Proverbs Used in Fables
## Form B

Name: _____  Date: _____

**Directions**

Fables are short stories that teach a lesson. The lesson in a fable is usually summarized in a statement called a *proverb*. A proverb is a single sentence that teaches a lesson or shows an example. Read and discuss the following fables. Notice that each fable ends with a proverb (shown in bold letters). Circle the letter of the best meaning for each proverb from the three choices provided. Be prepared to discuss your answers. Ask questions if you need assistance.

1. A boy put his hand into a bag full of marbles. He grasped as many as he could possibly hold, but when he tried to pull out his hand, he was prevented from doing so by the narrow opening of the bag. Unwilling to let go of any marbles, and yet unable to withdraw his hand with so many marbles in it, he burst into tears out of frustration. A bystander said to him, "Be satisfied with half the quantity, and you will be able to draw out your hand. Didn't your mother ever tell you **"Don't bite off more than you can chew?"**

   ***Don't bite off more than you can chew*** means:

   a. Marbles are impossible to hold.

   b. Do not attempt too much at once.

   c. Strangers cannot be trusted.

**Figurative Language**

2. A peacock spreading its gorgeous tail made fun of a crane that passed by. The peacock ridiculed the gray color of the crane's feathers and said, "I am robed, like a king, in gold and purple and all the colors of the rainbow, while you have not a bit of color on your wings." "True," replied the crane, "but I soar to the heights of heaven and lift up my voice to the stars, while you walk below, like a turtle, among the common creatures of the earth. **Fine feathers do not make fine birds.**"

*Fine feathers do not make fine birds* means:

    a.  Actions speak louder than words.

    b.  A peacock looks nice, but cannot fly like a crane.

    c.  How you appear is not a measure of who you are.

3. A fox caught in a trap escaped, but in so doing lost his tail. Thereafter, feeling his life a burden from the shame and ridicule of losing his tail, he planned to convince all the other foxes that being tailless was much more attractive. He gathered together a good many foxes and advised them to cut off their tails, saying that they would not only look much better without them, but that they would get rid of the excessive weight, which was a great inconvenience. One fox interrupted him and said, "If you had not yourself lost your tail, my friend, you would not be telling us that having no tail was better. **Misery loves company.**"

*Misery loves company* means:

    a.  Large companies make people miserable.

    b.  Unhappy people like to commiserate, instead of being happy for others.

    c.  A fox without a tail is miserable.

**Figurative Language** © 2002 Thinking Publications
Duplication permitted for educational use only.

*Chapter 4: Proverbs*

# Activity 1—
# Understanding Proverbs Used in Fables
## Form C

Name: _____  Date: _____

**Directions**

Fables are short stories that teach a lesson. The lesson in a fable is usually summarized in a statement called a *proverb*. A proverb is a single sentence that teaches a lesson or shows an example. Read and discuss the following fables. Notice that each fable ends with a proverb (shown in bold letters). Circle the letter of the best meaning for each proverb from the three choices provided. Be prepared to discuss your answers. Ask questions if you need assistance.

1. A farmer was driving a wagon along a country lane when the wheels sank down deep into a rut. The driver, angry and upset, stood looking at the wagon and did nothing but utter loud cries to Hercules (a man of strength) to come help him. Hercules appeared and addressed him saying, "Put your shoulders to the wheels, my man. Push with all your might, and never wish for help until you have done your best to help yourself. **Self-help is the best help.**"

    *Self-help is the best help* means:

    a. Depend on yourself.

    b. No one is good enough to help you.

    c. A farmer needs a strong horse to pull a wagon.

**Figurative Language**

2. Once there was a hippo who wanted to be a dancer. Each day she practiced spinning and turning and gliding her way through the jungle. All the other hippos giggled as they watched her practice. "You'll never be a dancer," they cried. "You look ridiculous!" The hippo ignored the others and was determined to keep up her daily practice. Soon the hippo moved with grace and ease around the jungle. She said, **"Satisfaction comes to those who make themselves happy."**

*Satisfaction comes to those who make themselves happy* means:

   a. Hippos can become dancers.

   b. You should never try to please others.

   c. Being happy with yourself matters most.

3. Two travelers were walking on the road together when a bear came out of the woods. Both travelers started to run toward a tree, but one stumbled and fell to the ground. The faster traveler made it up the tree, never looking back to see if his friend was all right. As the bear came near, the fallen traveler pretended to play dead. The bear sniffed the traveler on the ground, whispered in his ear, and left. The faster traveler then came down the tree and asked, "What did the bear whisper in your ear?" The slower traveler replied, **"Beware of fair-weather friends."**

*Beware of fair-weather friends* means:

   a. Bears never attack a dead person.

   b. Difficult times can test a true friendship.

   c. Long journeys in the winter should be done by car.

124

**Figurative Language** © 2002 Thinking Publications
Duplication permitted for educational use only.

*Chapter 4: Proverbs*

# Activity 1—
# Understanding Proverbs Used in Fables
## Answer Key

**Form A (pgs 119–120)**

1. a
2. a
3. b

**Form B (pgs 121–122)**

1. b
2. c
3. b

**Form C (pgs 123–124)**

1. a
2. c
3. b

Figurative Language

# Activity 1—Understanding Proverbs Used in Fables

## Extension Ideas

1. Have students write their own fables or modify existing fables. Encourage students to illustrate their fables.

2. Have students illustrate fables from Activity 1. Then ask students to explain the fable and their drawing to the class.

*Chapter 4: Proverbs*

# Activity 2—Proverb Matching

## Form A

Name: _____    Date: _____

### Directions

Read each short story. Place an *X* next to the proverb that sums up the main idea of the story. Then give an example of a similar situation that describes the proverb. Be prepared to discuss your answers. Ask questions if you need assistance.

**1** I never really appreciated my wonderful family until I went away to college. Our family dinners seemed like an out-of-date routine that I started to resent. Now that I'm eating alone in my room, or in a cafeteria with strangers, I wish I could be home for one of those family dinners again.

_____ A penny saved is a penny earned.

_____ Every cloud has a silver lining.

_____ Absence makes the heart grow fonder.

Give an example of a similar situation: _____

_____

**2** "I know that I left my keys on this counter. I can't believe that they are missing. I want everyone to stop what they are doing and look for those keys. Look everywhere. They have to be here, and I can't leave without them."

_____ Leave no stone unturned.

_____ Too many cooks spoil the broth.

_____ Actions speak louder than words.

Give an example of a similar situation: _____

_____

**Figurative Language** © 2002 Thinking Publications
Duplication permitted for educational use only.

127

**Figurative Language**

**3**  Haley and Matt met at the funeral of a mutual friend. Even though both of them were saddened by the sudden passing of their dear friend, they began to talk to each other about their feelings. Soon their friendship turned into a romance. If it hadn't been for the sad event of the funeral, they would have never met each other.

_____ Two wrongs do not make a right.

_____ Never put off until tomorrow what you can do today.

_____ Every cloud has a silver lining.

Give an example of a similar situation: _____

_____

**4**  Jill's next-door neighbor, Jack, had been very helpful to her with some home repairs that she needed. Jack fixed her garbage disposal and helped her put up a fence that was falling down. In return, Jill baked him some homemade bread and mended some kitchen curtains for him.

_____ A stitch in time saves nine.

_____ There are plenty of other fish in the sea.

_____ A kindness does not go unrewarded.

Give an example of a similar situation: _____

_____

**Figurative Language** © 2002 Thinking Publications
Duplication permitted for educational use only.

*Chapter 4: Proverbs*

# Activity 2—Proverb Matching
## Form B

Name: _____   Date: _____

### Directions

Read each short story. Place an *X* next to the proverb that sums up the main idea of the story. Then give an example of a similar situation that describes the proverb. Be prepared to discuss your answers. Ask questions if you need assistance.

**1** Fay was warned not to wear her new earrings into the shower. They were expensive, so her mother didn't want her to lose them. Fay was in a hurry and despite her mother's warnings, took a shower wearing the earrings. While in the shower, one earring went down the drain. Upset and crying, Fay told her mother, who said, "There's nothing you can do about it now. It's gone and you just have to accept it."

_____ There's no use crying over spilled milk.
_____ Curiosity killed the cat.
_____ All that glitters is not gold.

Give an example of a similar situation: _____

_____

**2** All the guys in the class were interested in dating Jen because she was beautiful. But after going out on a few dates with her, most of the guys decided not to call her back. They found her to be pushy and selfish and only interested in either talking about herself or having them buy her things. Jen may have had a beautiful face, but her personality needed some work.

_____ Haste makes waste.
_____ Beauty is only skin deep.
_____ Beggars can't be choosers.

Give an example of a similar situation: _____

_____

**Figurative Language** © 2002 Thinking Publications
Duplication permitted for educational use only.

129

**Figurative Language**

**3**

George could not wait to grow up. While still in high school, he applied for credit cards, tried to buy a car on his own, and wanted to open a checking account. He had a part-time job, but no bank would give him a line of credit or a checking account. The most they would give him was a savings account. This frustrated George, but he kept trying. Finally his mother told him, "Be patient. Some things take time. You don't get everything you want right away."

_____ Good things come to those who wait.

_____ A bird in the hand is worth two in the bush.

_____ The best things in life are free.

Give an example of a similar situation: _____

_____

**4**

Tim was good at getting jobs, but he couldn't seem to keep one for more than a few months. He always seemed to have arguments with other employees or even the manager. Finally, they'd end up telling him not to come back. He never told his future employers about his past jobs, because he knew they would not give him a good recommendation. One day, Tim was on an interview for a job he really wanted and he was asked for the phone number of his last employer. Tim suddenly realized how his past job performance could affect his future employment.

_____ Don't burn your bridges behind you.

_____ That's the way the cookie crumbles.

_____ Don't judge a book by its cover.

Give an example of a similar situation: _____

_____

**Figurative Language** © 2002 Thinking Publications
Duplication permitted for educational use only.

*Chapter 4: Proverbs*

# Activity 2—Proverb Matching
## Form C

Name: _____     Date: _____

### Directions

Read each short story. Place an *X* next to the proverb that sums up the main idea of the story. Then give an example of a similar situation that describes the proverb. Be prepared to discuss your answers. Ask questions if you need assistance.

**1** Rick kept looking at the oven and then the clock. The smell of the baking cake was making his mouth water. He asked his mom, "Are you sure the oven is working right? The cake doesn't look like it's baking." His mom said, "You have to stop looking at the oven; it won't bake any faster if you watch it. Go watch TV to take your mind off of that cake!"

_____ Look before you leap.
_____ A watched pot never boils.
_____ Never look a gift horse in the mouth.

Give an example of a similar situation: _____

_____

**2** Anthony liked to criticize his friends when they made a mistake. He always said that if the same thing had happened to him, he'd know exactly what to do. One day, Anthony tried to cheat on an exam and got caught. All of his friends were quick to remind him that he never makes any mistakes. They also told him they didn't want to hear any more of his criticisms about them, since he wasn't so perfect after all.

_____ Don't kill the goose that laid the golden egg.
_____ People who live in glass houses shouldn't throw stones.
_____ Let sleeping dogs lie.

Give an example of a similar situation:_____

_____

**Figurative Language** © 2002 Thinking Publications
Duplication permitted for educational use only.

**Figurative Language**

**3**  Tray always found trouble. If there was a fight at school, he was the first one there to see it. If he saw fire engines racing down the street, he followed them. One day, he followed a police car as it was on its way to a civil disturbance. Tray got too close to the action and was arrested. At the police station, Tray tried to explain why he was at the scene. The police officer said, "If you know there's trouble ahead, you should avoid it, not get closer to it."

_____  Where there's smoke, there's fire.

_____  A rolling stone gathers no moss.

_____  Where there's a will, there's a way.

Give an example of a similar situation: _____

_____

**4**  After Sandy had ordered her wedding gown and all the dresses for the bridesmaids, she saw some even prettier dresses. She wondered if she could change her order. After several phone calls, she found out she could change her order, but it was going to cost her more money and the bridesmaids dresses might not be ready by the wedding date. Finally, Sandy decided that she had better stick with her first choices, or else she may cause herself bigger problems.

_____  Every dog has his day.

_____  Put your money where your mouth is.

_____  Don't change horses midstream.

Give an example of a similar situation:_____

_____

**Figurative Language** © 2002 Thinking Publications
Duplication permitted for educational use only.

*Chapter 4: Proverbs*

# Activity 2—Proverb Matching
## Answer Key

**Form A (pgs 127–128)**

1. Absence makes the heart grow fonder.
2. Leave no stone unturned.
3. Every cloud has a silver lining.
4. A kindness does not go unrewarded

**Form B (pgs 129–130)**

1. There's no use crying over spilled milk.
2. Beauty is only skin deep.
3. Good things come to those who wait.
4. Don't burn your bridges behind you.

**Form C (pgs 131–132)**

1. A watched pot never boils.
2. People who live in glass houses shouldn't throw stones.
3. Where there's smoke, there's fire.
4. Don't change horses midstream.

**Figurative Language**

# Activity 2—Proverb Matching
## Extension Ideas

1. Direct students to be on the lookout for proverbs in various forms of media and in their academic resources. Encourage students to bring in the examples they find. Discuss the proverbs and their meanings as a group.

2. Have students give examples of situations that can describe some proverbs that are not discussed in the Activity 2 pages.

*Chapter 4: Proverbs*

# Activity 3—Understanding Proverbs
## Form A

Name: _____    Date: _____

### Directions

Proverbs sometimes teach us about virtues or ideals, such as courage, honesty, or love. (A virtue is an excellence or goodness. An ideal is an objective or ultimate goal.) Read each story below. At the end of each story is a proverb (shown in bold letters). Place an *X* next to the virtue or ideal that the proverb seems to highlight. Be prepared to discuss your answers. Ask questions if you need assistance.

**1** John was nothing more than a bully. He always picked on those who were weaker than him or who couldn't defend themselves. One day, John met his match. Tory, tired of being picked on and pushed around by John, decided to fight back. At first, Tory didn't know if he could overpower John, but he decided that enough was enough. Three good blows, and John ran away from Tory as fast as he could. **A bully is always a coward.**

This proverb highlights:

_____ courage          _____ honesty          _____ friendship

**2** Mia had a lot of friends. Then she got cancer. Mia was very sick during the chemotherapy treatments. Most of her friends stopped calling, except for one: Judy. Judy came to see her in the hospital and came to her house to see how she was doing. Judy brought Mia her homework and copied her notes for Mia so she could keep up with her classwork when she was feeling better. Judy even bought her a really cool hat to wear when Mia's hair fell out. Mia realized how lucky she was to know a great person like Judy. **A friend in need is a friend indeed.**

This proverb highlights:

_____ wisdom          _____ friendship          _____ security

**Figurative Language** © 2002 Thinking Publications
Duplication permitted for educational use only.

135

**Figurative Language**

**3** Jerry saved money each week from his paycheck. As his savings grew, he invested some of it in stocks and bonds. Some people said that Jerry should spend some of his money and enjoy himself. Jerry knew that saving money now was important for the future, and having something for the future gave him satisfaction. **A heavy purse makes a light heart.**

This proverb highlights:

_____ love                    _____ honesty                    _____ security

**4** Susana and Debra have been friends since high school. Some thought that they were more like sisters than friends. One day someone asked Susana if she and Debra ever had any disagreements or fights. She said, "Not really, but we are both careful to respect each other's space and not take anything for granted." She added, "If either of us is getting on the other's nerves, we just leave each other alone for a while. **A hedge between keeps friendship green.**"

This proverb highlights:

_____ loyalty                 _____ friendship                 _____ courage

**5** There is a new political party forming called the People's Party. I am really interested in following its formation. The problem is that the people involved with it can't agree on what they should stand for, the issues they should support, or even who should be their candidate. From what I can tell, all they are doing is arguing with each other. Because of the bickering, I don't think they will be able to get organized and get the party off the ground. **A house divided cannot stand.**

This proverb highlights:

_____ loyalty                 _____ security                  _____ generosity

**Figurative Language** © 2002 Thinking Publications
Duplication permitted for educational use only.

136

*Chapter 4: Proverbs*

# Activity 3—Understanding Proverbs
## Form B

Name: _____ Date: _____

| Directions |
| --- |

Proverbs sometimes teach us about virtues or ideals, such as courage, honesty, or love. (A virtue is an excellence or goodness. An ideal is an objective or ultimate goal.) Read each story below. At the end of each story is a proverb (shown in bold letters). Place an *X* next to the virtue or ideal that the proverb seems to highlight. Be prepared to discuss your answers. Ask questions if you need assistance.

1. Laura was known to be hard to please and highly critical of others. One day her friend Wayne, in trying to surprise and impress Laura, put a beautiful card and a box of expensive chocolates in her locker. Upon discovering them, Laura commented, "Does he really think I'm going to eat this junk?" Wayne overheard her remark and was crushed. Laura, feeling badly about what she had just said, ran after Wayne and tried to explain what she really meant, but it was too late. **A word once spoken is past recalling.**

   This proverb highlights:

   _____ trust          _____ courage          _____ regret

2. Everyone in the neighborhood knew that Bobby was the first to get out of hand at a party. Some suspected that he had a real problem with alcohol. The rest of the time, he was a great neighbor and friend. The annual 4th of July block party was coming up, and the menu and refreshments were being discussed by some of the neighbors. One neighbor suggested that all the drinks be nonalcoholic, for Bobby's sake. **Better safe than sorry.**

   This proverb highlights:

   _____ truth          _____ wisdom          _____ courage

**Figurative Language** © 2002 Thinking Publications
Duplication permitted for educational use only.

**Figurative Language**

**3** I tried to warn Rochelle to stay away from Darrin. He was suddenly being nice to her, calling her at night, and buying her lunch. Before this, he wouldn't even say hello to her. I said, "If he's being so nice all of the sudden, there must be a reason." Sure enough, the next day Darrin asked Rochelle to do his English research project for him. I just knew **he was a wolf in sheep's clothing.**

This proverb highlights:

_____ generosity          _____ revenge          _____ trust

**4** Lately I noticed that my friend Denice was quiet and looking sad. I asked her if she was feeling all right, but she would just brush me off and say she was fine. I sensed that something was really wrong. I told her that I noticed she hadn't been herself for the last several days and asked her to please tell me what was wrong. Denice said, "I really don't want to bother you with my troubles. Besides, you couldn't really do anything about it anyway." I said, "I  don't know if I can help you, but telling someone what's bothering you can make you feel better. You can't solve all your problems alone. **A trouble shared is a trouble halved.**"

This proverb highlights:

_____ friendship          _____ responsibility          _____ hard work

**5** Samuel was upset about the rabbits that were invading his garden and eating all of his prized vegetables. He worked hard to get them to grow and was furious that these critters were now eating all of his hard work. He decided that he would set a trap for them. He put some of his vegetables out on the ground and sprinkled them with poison. Samuel said, "If they want to eat my vegetables, then they will pay. **An eye for an eye, a tooth for a tooth.**"

This proverb highlights:

_____ honesty          _____ courage          _____ revenge

*Chapter 4: Proverbs*

# Activity 3—Understanding Proverbs
## Form C

Name: _____    Date: _____

### Directions

Proverbs sometimes teach us about virtues or ideals, such as courage, honesty, or love. (A virtue is an excellence or goodness. An ideal is an objective or ultimate goal.) Read each story below. At the end of each story is a proverb (shown in bold letters). Place an *X* next to the virtue or ideal that the proverb seems to highlight. Be prepared to discuss your answers. Ask questions if you need assistance.

1. Stephan had stayed at the mall later than he realized. It was getting dark and he had to take the bus home. While waiting for the bus, the sky grew dark and it started to pour. He couldn't go back to the mall, because it was closed, so he looked around for another dry place to wait. He saw a bar across the street and decided to go there. Once inside, it smelled bad and was dirty. The customers gave him a suspicious look. Stephan said, "I'm just waiting for the next bus." He knew the bar wasn't the best place to wait, but he had no choice. **Any port in a storm.**

This proverb highlights:

_____ patience            _____ safety            _____ hard work

2. The jury had to decide if T.J. was guilty of robbing a convenience store. He pleaded "Not guilty," but there were witnesses and evidence that indicated otherwise. What really convinced the jury was the videotape of T.J. holding a gun and taking money out of the cash register. It was him, **beyond a shadow of a doubt.**

This proverb highlights:

_____ truth            _____ courage            _____ patience

**Figurative Language** © 2002 Thinking Publications
Duplication permitted for educational use only.

139

**Figurative Language**

**3** Jaymie was always telling us exaggerated stories. If we were talking about a movie star, he would tell us he had met that star. If we were talking about some far-away place, of course, Jaymie had been there. He even told us he was related to a famous princess, but didn't know her name! One day, Jaymie announced that he was moving to Canada. No one believed him. He kept insisting that he was moving, but none of us listened. When he wasn't in school for a few days, we got curious and went to the office. When we asked where Jaymie was, we were told he had transferred to a school in Toronto. Since we didn't believe Jaymie, we never got a chance to say goodbye to him. **Never cry "Wolf!"**

This proverb highlights:

_____ honesty _____ friendship _____ courage

**4** Travis wanted to work for a really big corporation. He knew he didn't have all the experience he needed, but he kept applying for jobs there, anytime an opening was advertised. Finally, a manager called him in for an interview. Travis impressed him with his enthusiasm and knowledge of the company. The manager said he would hire him, and Travis started work the next day. **Constant dripping wears away a stone.**

This proverb highlights:

_____ independence _____ persistence _____ honesty

**5** Bryan's mother said it was time for her son to be out on his own. He was 24, had a good job with benefits, and a car. It was time for him to move out and get his own place. He could afford it, and he needed to get on with his life. She told him, "You need to support yourself and live on your own now. **Every tub stands on its own feet.**"

This proverb highlights:

_____ friendship _____ kindness _____ independence

**Figurative Language** © 2002 Thinking Publications
Duplication permitted for educational use only.

140

# Activity 3—Understanding Proverbs
## Answer Key

**Form A (pgs 135–136)**
1. courage
2. friendship
3. security
4. friendship
5. loyalty

**Form B (pgs 137–138)**
1. regret
2. wisdom
3. trust
4. friendship
5. revenge

**Form C (pgs 139–140)**
1. safety
2. truth
3. honesty
4. persistence
5. independence

**Figurative Language**

# Activity 3— Understanding Proverbs
## Extension Ideas

1. Encourage students to use online literature sources such as

    - *http://www.2020site.org/aesop*
    - *http://geocities.com/fables312*
    - *http://www.dusklight.com*

    to locate and define fables and proverbs they encounter.

2. Challenge students to write proverb stories when there are a few spare minutes of class remaining. Keep a collection of these stories in a class journal.

*Chapter 4: Proverbs*

# Activity 4—Explaining Proverbs
## Form A

Name: _____     Date: _____

### Directions

Read each short story. Then write or tell your explanation of the proverb (shown in bold letters). Be prepared to discuss your answers. Ask questions if you need assistance.

**1** ▷ The time is right to start my own Internet business. I know what I have to do to get started, and I have researched the market and my product. I know that this business has a very good chance of succeeding. If I wait any longer, the market will be too crowded to get in. I should **strike while the iron is hot.**

This proverb means: _____

_____

_____

_____

**2** ▷ Tara cashed her first paycheck and headed straight to the mall. She was so excited about having her own money that she began buying things without thinking about the cost. After about an hour, she reached into her wallet and realized she was out of money. She couldn't believe she had spent it all so fast. Tara was embarrassed to have been so careless with her first paycheck. Now she'd have to wait two weeks before she could buy anything else. It's like they say: **A fool and his money are soon parted.**

This proverb means: _____

_____

_____

_____

**Figurative Language** © 2002 Thinking Publications
Duplication permitted for educational use only.

143

**Figurative Language**

**3** Jason was in trouble from the time he was a young boy in elementary school. He was in and out of detention centers all through middle school and high school. He wound up getting into so much trouble with the law that he was sent to prison for five years. We all thought we had seen the last of him in this town, but my aunt said, "Just wait. That kind of kid always comes back to where he started from. **A bad penny always turns up.**"

This proverb means: _____

_____

_____

_____

**4** Our American History teacher is always complaining about how lazy everyone is in our class, and at least once a week he threatens to fail all of us. He makes a big deal out of students who use the restroom too often or who forget their homework. Even though he is constantly reminding us that we are going to get *F*s, he never gives them to us. **His bark is worse than his bite.**

This proverb means: _____

_____

_____

_____

**5** Dylan's drunk-driving accident almost killed him. It got him to realize how lucky he was to still be alive. After months of recovery from his injuries, he stopped drinking. He straightened out his life by becoming more responsible, before he killed himself or someone else. I guess his car accident was really **a blessing in disguise.**

This proverb means: _____

_____

_____

_____

**Figurative Language** © 2002 Thinking Publications
Duplication permitted for educational use only.

144

*Chapter 4: Proverbs*

# Activity 4—Explaining Proverbs
## Form B

Name: _____     Date: _____

| Directions |
|---|

Read each short story. Then write or tell your explanation of the proverb (shown in bold letters). Be prepared to discuss your answers. Ask questions if you need assistance.

**1** Tony's mother kept hinting to him that he should get a job and stop hanging around the house. Tony always told her he was working on it, but he never actually did anything. Finally, his mother got mad and told him to get out, shouting, "Don't come back unless you have a job!" Tony's mom was sorry she had to yell, but **a cat in gloves catches no mice."**

This proverb means: _____

_____

_____

_____

**2** It would have been a perfect crime. There were no witnesses and no way to trace Raymond to the stolen goods. But Raymond couldn't stop thinking about what he had done, or what his family would think if they knew what he had done. He finally went to the police and confessed. **A guilty conscience needs no accuser.**

This proverb means: _____

_____

_____

_____

**Figurative Language** © 2002 Thinking Publications
Duplication permitted for educational use only.

145

**Figurative Language**

**3** Chris always treats his girlfriend Roxanne well. He sends her flowers, takes her to the movies, and sends her cards. Every day, Roxanne makes lunch for Chris and brings it to school for him. **A good Jack makes a good Jill.**

This proverb means: _____

_____

_____

_____

**4** No one knows how Kayla keeps up with all of her activities. She is always prepared for class, has her homework done, and has even read the next chapter or assignment. She gets *A*s and usually scores the highest on tests. She also manages to hold down a part-time job and run cross-country. Kayla says, "Studies are my priority. I just sit down and do it. That way I have time for the other things I want to do. But studying always comes first." Kayla knows that learning is work and **there is no royal road to learning.**

This proverb means: _____

_____

_____

_____

**5** Jenna didn't lie about the scratch in her mother's car; she just didn't tell her mother that she was the one who did it. By not saying anything, Jenna let her mom think that someone else had done it. **There's a sin of omission as well as commission.**

This proverb means: _____

_____

_____

_____

146

# Activity 4—
# Explaining Proverbs
## Extension Ideas

1. Have students circle or highlight the Activity 4 words from the context that gave them clues to the meaning of each proverb. Then have students explain why they picked those words as clues.

2. Have students retell the proverb stories in Activity 4 using their own words. Encourage students to make additional changes to the stories, using new characters and settings as possible.

Figurative Language

# Activity 5— Proverbs Card Game

### Directions

Create a proverbs card deck. Choose from the proverbs provided below, or use proverbs from students' classroom curriculum and daily lives. For each example, write the proverb on one side of a 3" × 5" index card and the meaning on the other side of the card. If possible, have students help create the card deck.

Group students into two teams. Place the deck with the meanings facedown in the center of a table. Have teams take turns choosing the top card from the deck and saying the proverb aloud to the other team. The responding team must then state the meaning of the given proverb. If the responding team is successful, they keep the card. If the responding team is not successful, the card should be returned to the bottom of the deck. The team with the most cards at the end wins.

NOTE: As another option, write the proverbs on one set of cards and the meanings on another set of cards. Then use the two decks to play a classic game of Memory by having students match the proverbs to their meanings.

| Proverb | Meaning |
| --- | --- |
| United we stand, divided we fall. | If you work together, you will have a stronger defense than working alone. |
| No man is an island. | We all need help from others from time to time. |
| One good turn deserves another. | Help someone else, and one day you, too, will be helped. |
| Don't bite off more than you can chew. | Do not attempt too much at once. |
| Fine feathers do not make fine birds. | How you appear is not who you are. |
| Misery loves company. | Unhappy people like to commiserate, instead of being happy for others. |
| Self-help is the best help. | Depend on yourself. |

| Proverb | Meaning |
|---|---|
| Satisfaction comes to those who make themselves happy. | Being happy with yourself matters most. |
| Beware of fair-weather friends. | Difficult times can test a true friendship. |
| Absence makes the heart grow fonder. | You'll probably miss something once you no longer have it in your life. |
| Leave no stone unturned. | Look everywhere. |
| Every cloud has a silver lining. | Something that at first seems bad might turn out to be good. |
| A kindness does not go unrewarded. | Helping someone else will one day be rewarded with help. |
| There's no use crying over spilled milk. | Don't be upset about things you cannot control. |
| Beauty is only skin deep. | A beautiful person may not have a beautiful personality. |
| Good things come to those who wait. | People who wait patiently for their reward are often rewarded. |
| Don't burn your bridges behind you. | Don't leave yourself with no connection to where you came from. |
| A watched pot never boils. | Time goes slowly when you are waiting for something. |
| People who live in glass houses shouldn't throw stones. | People with faults shouldn't criticize others. |
| Where there's smoke, there's fire. | If there's some trouble, there's usually a lot more. |
| Don't change horses midstream. | Don't make changes in the middle of a project. |
| A bully is always a coward. | A bully cannot fight an equal, so he intimidates the weak. |
| A friend in need is a friend indeed. | A friend in times of trouble is a true friend. |
| A heavy purse makes a light heart. | Having money makes you feel secure. |
| A hedge between keeps friendship green. | Having privacy keeps a friendship healthy. |
| A house divided cannot stand. | People need to work together to accomplish things. |
| A word once spoken is past recalling. | You cannot take back something you just said. |
| Better safe than sorry. | Better to be very careful than to make a mistake. |

**Figurative Language**

| Proverb | Meaning |
|---|---|
| He was a wolf in sheep's clothing. | He was a person who tried to be seen as a friend, but he was actually an enemy. |
| A trouble shared is a trouble halved. | Telling someone your troubles means they might help you solve them. |
| An eye for an eye, a tooth for a tooth. | If you harm someone or something, the same should happen to you. |
| Any port in a storm. | When in trouble, you might have to seek help from somewhere you normally would not go. |
| Beyond a shadow of a doubt. | Being absolutely certain. |
| Never cry "Wolf!" | Don't tell lies or people won't believe you when you're actually telling the truth. |
| Constant dripping wears away a stone. | Persistence will help you achieve your goal. |
| Every tub stands on its own feet. | Be independent. |
| Strike while the iron is hot. | If you have a chance to do something, do it or you will lose your chance. |
| A fool and his money are soon parted. | A foolish person will spend his or her money unwisely. |
| A bad penny always turns up. | A troublemaker seems to keep making himself or herself known. |
| His bark is worse than his bite. | Someone always makes threats, but he or she seldom carries them out. |
| A blessing in disguise. | Something good can come out of a bad situation. |
| A cat in gloves catches no mice. | You cannot always get what you want by being careful and polite. |
| A guilty conscience needs no accuser. | Feeling guilty will make you want to confess. |
| A good Jack makes a good Jill. | If a man treats a woman well, she will treat him well in return. |
| There is no royal road to learning. | Learning is hard work. |
| There's a sin of omission as well as commission. | Failing to do something can be as bad as doing something wrong. |

150

# Humor
## (Riddles and Jokes)
### Chapter 5

## What Is Humor?

Humor is not easily defined, although most people recognize it when they hear or see it. In general, humor involves an incongruity or a mismatch of ideas that triggers a humorous response, such as smiling or laughing (Gardner et al., 1978). Understanding humor requires the listener or reader to go beyond the literal interpretation of the words and find meaning in what is not directly stated (Bernstein, 1986). Humor has linguistic and nonlinguistic features and can occur in both spoken and written form. The most common forms of humor are riddles and jokes. Riddles rely on linguistic ambiguity and usually follow a question-and-answer format. Jokes are similar to riddles because they also rely on some form of linguistic ambiguity. A joke can be understood and appreciated only when the ambiguity is figured out. Riddles and jokes are similar to metaphors, idioms, and proverbs because they require us to suspend our literal interpretations and appreciate the unexpected (Lund and Duchan, 1988).

## Review of the Literature

Some aspects of humor have been well documented, while others have remained relatively unexplored. Humor research has not always been viewed as serious or legitimate work. Because of the persistence of several researchers, though, humor is now viewed as a useful index of cognitive development (Bernstein, 1986). Considerable research has focused on the development of children's understanding of humor (Spector, 1990), and some research has centered on the linguistic aspects of riddles and jokes (e.g., Gardner et al., 1978).

**Figurative Language**

For adolescents, the ability to understand and use humor is a prized ability. Kutner (1988) explained that adolescents use humor to define their membership in a social group. The ones that understand its humor belong; the ones who don't are outsiders.

Finally, Ziv (1976) pointed out that discriminate use of humor by an instructor can contribute to a relaxed classroom atmosphere, reduce social anxiety, and increase group cohesiveness. Bryant and Zillmann (1989) concluded that the judicious use of humor by classroom teachers can promote creativity, improve attention, and make learning more enjoyable for students. These researchers also caution against the use of sarcasm and ridicule as harmful and destructive forms of language.

# Developmental Information

The developmental aspects of humor appear to be similar to other forms of figurative language. In humor, comprehension precedes production and explanation (McGhee, 1971a, 1971b, 1971c; McGhee and Chapman, 1980). McGhee (1971a, 1971b, 1971c) indicated that concrete operational thought (ages 7–12 years) is needed for linguistic humor comprehension. In addition, Fowles and Glanz (1977) found that humor competence of riddles and jokes was more closely related to reading ability than age.

The development of the comprehension of various riddle types has been identified by several researchers (e.g., Fowles and Glanz, 1977; Schultz, 1974). Table 5.1 summarizes the development of riddle types and provides examples of each type. Joke types and their development have also been identified by several researchers (e.g., Bernstein, 1986; Fowles and Glanz, 1977; Hirsh-Pasek, Gleitman and Gleitman, 1978; Lund and Duchan, 1988; Schultz and Horibe, 1974). Table 5.2 (on page 154) summarizes this development and provides examples of each joke type.

# How Can This Chapter Be Used?

There are five activities in Chapter 5. For most students, begin with Activity 1 and move through the activities in the order provided. While the difficulty of each type of task gets progressively more challenging, the difficulty of the riddles and jokes within each type of task varies for each activity. It is recommended that the card game described in Activity 5 be conducted after students have been exposed to the preceding activities within the chapter. Survey the riddles and jokes within each activity for appropriateness of use. Tables 5.1 and 5.2 can be useful for identifying the types of riddles and jokes that are developmentally appropriate for your students.

152

*Chapter 5: Humor*

| Table 5.1 | Development of Riddle Types | | |
|---|---|---|---|
| **Age of Comprehension** | **Type of Humor** | **Definition** | **Example** |
| 6–9 years | Phonological | Similar sounding words with more than one meaning | **Q.** Why did the cookie cry? <br> **A.** Because his mother had been a wafer so long. |
| 6–15 years | Lexical | Multiple-meaning words | **Q.** What's black and white and red all over? <br> **A.** A newspaper. |
| 10–12 years | Surface | Altered groups of word segments | **Q.** What has four wheels and flies? <br> **A.** A garbage truck. |
| 12 years | Deep | Different interpretations for the same sentence | **Q.** What's the difference between a running dog and a running man? <br> **A.** The man wears trousers and the dog pants. |
| 12$^+$ years | Metalinguistic | The form of language, not the meaning, is important | **Q.** How do you spell this? <br> **A.** *t–h–i–s* |

*Sources:* Fowles and Glanz (1977); Schultz (1974)

- **Activity 1** targets understanding of riddles through a multiple-choice task format. For this activity students are asked to choose the "funny" punchline for each provided riddle. Form A and Form B are provided for Activity 1, as is an answer key and extension ideas.

- **Activity 2** is a multiple-choice task, but jokes rather than riddles are the target. For these tasks, students are asked to choose the best ending for each joke. Activity 2 includes Form A, Form B, an answer key, and extension ideas.

- **Activity 3** challenges students to choose the best ending for each joke. One form is provided for Activity 3, along with an answer key and extension ideas.

153

**Figurative Language**

| Table 5.2 | | Development of Joke Types | |
|---|---|---|---|
| **Age of Comprehension** | **Type of Humor** | **Definition** | **Example** |
| <6 years | Nonlinguistic | Visual humor; humor not involving language | Cartoons without captions |
| 6–8 years | Phonological | Similar sounding words with more than one meaning | **Q.** If you have three ducks in a box, what do you have? **A.** A box of quackers. |
| 8–10 years | Lexical | Multiple-meaning words | **JUDGE:** Order in the court! **ATTORNEY:** I'll take a large sausage pizza. |
| 10–12 years | Surface | Altered groups of word segments | **HENRY:** I saw a man-eating shark in the aquarium. **JACK:** That's nothing. I saw a man eating herring in the cafe. |
| 10–12 years | Deep | Different interpretations for the same sentence | **JILL:** Call me a cab. **BILL:** Okay, you're a cab. |
| 12⁺ years | Metalinguistic | The form of language, not the meaning, is important | **Q.** What is at the end of everything? **A.** The letter *g*. |

*Sources:* Bernstein (1986); Fowles and Glanz (1977); Hirsh-Pasek et al. (1978); Lund and Duchan (1988); Schultz and Horibe (1974)

- **Activity 4** presents funny stories (adapted from Perret, 1991) and asks students to explain the linguistic humor in each story. Activity 4 includes one form and with extension ideas.

- **Activity 5** presents directions and a list of riddles and jokes for creating a card game to target students' understanding and use of humor. (Also consider using appropriate riddles and jokes from students' daily lives for this activity.)

For all five activities, encourage students to talk about the possible meanings of each riddle and joke as the tasks are discussed and completed. Also, direct students to read the tasks aloud to help them better recognize whether their response is accurate. Help students understand how to use context cues in order to figure out the meaning of riddles and jokes. In addition, refer to "Suggested Adaptations" (page 7) for optional reading and writing adaptations.

Consider these activity pages as lesson or discussion guides rather than as paper-and-pencil tasks. Bridge discussions by talking about when students might encounter the given riddles and jokes in their personal lives.

---

## A Word of Caution

Humor has important social implications. For adolescents, it can mean acceptance with peers, which is critical for them at this stage of their lives. When humor is appropriately used by an instructor, it can contribute to a relaxed learning environment for students (Ziv, 1976). However, humor that contains sexist, prejudiced, or offensive language should not be used. Any language that might be viewed as a putdown by any group should not be used. A good rule of thumb is that if you have to think twice about the intended meaning of a joke or riddle, don't use it. In addition, monitor students' use of humor to ensure that it does not become a means for ridiculing others. Class rules and limits need to be established before beginning this chapter on humor. You may also need to inform parents and appropriate school staff of the purpose of covering this form of figurative language and the class rules and limits for the activities in this chapter. Careful planning will ensure that the activities are fully enjoyed by all students.

Figurative Language

# Activity 1—Understanding Riddles
## Form A

Name: _____   Date: _____

**Directions**

Riddles use words in a special way to make a funny statement. For each riddle below, read the question and the two corresponding answer options. Use the words in bold letters as clues to help you choose the answer that makes the riddle funny. Circle that answer. The funny answer will be the one that is unusual or that surprises you. The wrong answer might be true, but it won't be funny. Be prepared to discuss your answers. Ask questions if you need assistance.

1. **Q.** Why did the woman take a **bath** with her **shirt on**?

    **A.** The label said "wash and wear."

    OR

    **A.** She was in a hurry.

2. **Q.** How do you make a **band stand**?

    **A.** Out of wood.

    OR

    **A.** Take away their chairs.

3. **Q.** What does a **cat** eat for **breakfast**?

    **A.** Cat food.

    OR

    **A.** Mice Crispies.

Figurative Language © 2002 Thinking Publications
Duplication permitted for educational use only.

*Chapter 5: Humor*

4. **Q.** What do you call a **bee** that **drops things?**

   **A.** A fumble bee.

   OR

   **A.** Clumsy.

5. **Q.** What do you get when you cross a **chicken** with a **desert?**

   **A.** A hot bird.

   OR

   **A.** Fried chicken.

6. **Q.** Why did the **turkey eat** so **fast?**

   **A.** He was a gobbler.

   OR

   **A.** He was really hungry.

7. **Q.** What goes **up** and never comes **down?**

   **A.** Air.

   OR

   **A.** Your age.

8. **Q.** Why did the **hot dog shiver?**

   **A.** It was covered with chili beans.

   OR

   **A.** It was in the freezer.

**Figurative Language** © 2002 Thinking Publications
Duplication permitted for educational use only.

157

Figurative Language

# Activity 1—Understanding Riddles
## Form B

Name: _____  Date: _____

> **Directions**
>
> Riddles use words in a special way to make a funny statement. For each riddle below, read the question and the two corresponding answer options. Use the words in bold letters as clues to help you choose the answer that makes the riddle funny. Circle that answer. The funny answer will be the one that is unusual or that surprises you. The wrong answer might be true, but it won't be funny. Be prepared to discuss your answers. Ask questions if you need assistance.

1. **Q.** What kind of **tables** do people **eat?**

   **A.** Vegetables.

   OR

   **A.** Small tables.

2. **Q.** Why did the **chicken cross the book?**

   **A.** The get to the author side.

   OR

   **A.** To go home.

3. **Q.** Why does the **Statue of Liberty stand** in New York Harbor?

   **A.** Because she's a statue.

   OR

   **A.** Because she can't sit down.

*Chapter 5: Humor*

4. **Q.** How do **amoebas talk** to each other?

   **A.** With their mouths.

   OR

   **A.** With their cell phones.


5. **Q.** What kind of **cheese doesn't belong** to you?

   **A.** Nacho cheese.

   OR

   **A.** Stolen cheese.


6. **Q.** What kind of **bug** is a **musical** bug?

   **A.** A bee.

   OR

   **A.** A humbug.


7. **Q.** Where do **bunnies** catch the **bus?**

   **A.** At the bus hop.

   OR

   **A.** At school.


8. **Q.** What do you get when you cross **snow** with a **tiger?**

   **A.** A cold tiger.

   OR

   **A.** Frostbite.

**Figurative Language** © 2002 Thinking Publications
Duplication permitted for educational use only.

**Figurative Language**

# Activity 1—Understanding Riddles
## Answer Key

**Form A (pgs 156–157)**

1. The label said "wash and wear."
2. Take away their chairs.
3. Mice Crispies.
4. A fumble bee.
5. Fried chicken.
6. He was a gobbler.
7. Your age.
8. It was covered with chili beans.

**Form B (pgs 158–159)**

1. Vegetables.
2. To get to the author side.
3. Because she can't sit down.
4. With their cell phones.
5. Nacho cheese.
6. A humbug.
7. At the bus hop.
8. Frostbite.

*Chapter 5: Humor*

# Activity 1—
# Understanding Riddles
## Extension Ideas

1. Have students explain how the words in bold in Activity 1 helped them figure out the correct answer for each riddle.

2. Have students locate riddles from a joke book or other resource (e.g., on the Web at a site like *http://www.kidsjokes.co.uk)*. Have students illustrate and share their riddles.

Figurative Language

# Activity 2—Understanding Jokes
## Form A

Name: _____   Date: _____

### Directions

Jokes are a form of humor. Read each joke. Then circle the letter of the answer that is the best explanation of why the joke is funny. Be prepared to discuss your answers. Ask questions if you need assistance.

**TOMAS:** Where can you find elephants?

**JUAN:** Anywhere. They're hard to hide.

This joke is funny because:

a. Juan didn't understand that Tomas was actually asking where elephants live.

b. Juan had no idea where elephants live, so he took a wild guess.

**LAURA:** Can you tell me how long pot roast should be cooked?

**TAMARA:** The same as short pot roast.

This joke is funny because:

a. Laura and Tamara know nothing about cooking pot roast.

b. Tamara thought the word *long* meant the size of the roast, not the length of the time needed to cook it.

*Figurative Language* © 2002 Thinking Publications
Duplication permitted for educational use only.

162

Chapter 5: Humor

**LIBRARIAN:** Did you enjoy reading *The Hunchback of Notre Dame?*
**STUDENT:** No, I read the first 100 pages, then I realized it wasn't about football.

This joke is funny because:

   a. The librarian was being kind to ask about the book.

   b. It took so long for the student to realize the subject of the book.

**TEACHER:** Shannon, give me a sentence that is a question.
**SHANNON:** Why do I get all the hard ones?
**TEACHER:** Very good.

This joke is funny because:

   a. Shannon answered the teacher without even realizing it.

   b. Shannon is always complaining to her teacher.

**JODI:** Are we having burgers on the grill tonight?
**MOM:** No, I think they're easier to eat on plates!

This joke is funny because:

   a. Jodi's mom doesn't have any clean dishes to use for dinner.

   b. Jodi's mom was talking about how they would eat the burgers, but Jodi was asking about where they would cook them.

**STUDENT:** Is there life after death?
**TEACHER:** Why do you ask?
**STUDENT:** I may need the extra time to finish all this homework you gave us.

This joke is funny because:

   a. The student does not want to do the homework the teacher assigned.

   b. The student found an unusual way to tell the teacher that the homework will take a lot of time to finish.

*Figurative Language* © 2002 Thinking Publications
Duplication permitted for educational use only.

Figurative Language

# Activity 2—Understanding Jokes
## Form B

Name: _____    Date: _____

### Directions

Jokes are a form of humor. Read each joke. Then circle the letter of the answer that is the best explanation of why the joke is funny. Be prepared to discuss your answers. Ask questions if you need assistance.

1. JASON: Would you ever yell at me for something I didn't do?

   DAD: Of course not. Why do you ask?

   JASON: Well, I didn't study for my test today.

   This joke is funny because:

   a. Jason tried to trick his father into not yelling at him.

   b. Jason knew he was going to get in trouble for his bad test grade.

2. NATALIA: How do they keep flies out of the cafeteria?

   CHEN: I don't know. How do they keep flies out of the cafeteria?

   NATALIA: Let them taste the food.

   This joke is funny because:

   a. Natalia was exaggerating about how bad the cafeteria food tasted.

   b. Natalia never eats lunch in the cafeteria; she goes home for lunch instead.

Chapter 5: Humor

SAM: We never have any food fights in our cafeteria.
PAM: Why, because it makes a mess?
SAM: No, because someone might accidentally swallow the food.

This joke is funny because:

a. The cafeteria food is well liked by the students.

b. Sam is exaggerating about how bad the food is.

DANIEL: The moon doesn't look hungry tonight.
DEBBIE: How can you tell?
DANIEL: Because it's full!

This joke is funny because:

a. Daniel was using the words *hungry* and *full* in an unexpected way.

b. Daniel likes to study the moon and stars and wants to be an astronomer.

DARRYL: Every morning I dream that I'm falling from a 15-story building, but just before I hit the ground, I wake up.
SHERYL: That's awful. What are you going to do about it?
DARRYL: Start dreaming about a 20-story building. I need more sleep!

This joke is funny because:

a. Darryl suggests that if he dreams of a taller building, he will have a longer fall during his dream, and then he'll be able to sleep longer.

b. Darryl should see a doctor if his bad dreams persist.

CUSTOMER: I'd like to try on that dress in the window.
CLERK: I'm sorry, but you'll have to change in the dressing room like everyone else.

This joke is funny because:

a. The salesperson thought the customer wanted to get dressed in the window.

b. The salesperson does not know how to deal with difficult customers.

**Figurative Language**

# Activity 2—Understanding Jokes
## Answer Key

**Form A (pgs 162–163)**

1. a
2. b
3. b
4. a
5. b
6. b

**Form B (pgs 164–165)**

1. a
2. a
3. b
4. a
5. a
6. a

# Activity 2— Understanding Jokes
## Extension Ideas

1. Have students underline or highlight the words in each Activity 2 joke that helped them interpret the exaggeration or absurdity that made the joke funny. Discuss why students chose the words and how these words acted as cues to the humor.

2. Have students create their own three-frame cartoon strips that tell a joke. Show students an example like the one below. Allow students to create their own jokes or to illustrate one that is provided in Activity 2. Encourage students to use as simple or as elaborate of an art style as they are comfortable with. Then have students share their cartoon jokes with each other.

**Sample**

167

Figurative Language

# Activity 3— Completing Funny Exaggerations

Name: _____  Date: _____

**Directions**

An exaggeration is a statement that makes something seem like more than it really is. Many times, an exaggeration causes something to be funny. Complete each joke by circling the letter of the answer that makes the joke funny. The funny answer will be the one that is unusual or that surprises you. The wrong answer might be true, but it won't be funny. Be prepared to discuss your answers. Ask questions if you need assistance.

**CARLOS:** I'm so hungry.
**JUANITA:** How hungry are you?

**CARLOS:** a. I'm so hungry I could eat my lunch.
b. I'm so hungry I could eat a horse.

**COLIN:** I'm so hot.
**QUINN:** How hot are you?

**COLIN:** a. I'm so hot I'm sweating.
b. I'm so hot you could fry an egg on my head.

**TIM:** The fog was so thick.
**JIM:** How thick was it?

**TIM:** a. It was so thick I could cut it with a knife.
b. It was so thick I couldn't see.

168

Chapter 5: Humor

MARIE: Jamie is so thin.
BARRY: How thin is she?

MARIE: a. She's so thin she wears a size 2.
b. She's so thin you could slide her under the door.

MICHAEL: I was so mad.
MAX: How mad were you?

MICHAEL: a. I was so mad I started to scream.
b. I was so mad steam came pouring out of my ears.

PHIL: I stood in line so long.
MIMI: How long did you stand in line?

PHIL: a. I stood in line so long I had another birthday.
b. I stood in line so long my feet started to ache.

GAIL: He screamed so loud.
STEVEN: How loud did he scream?

GAIL: a. He screamed so loud it hurt my ears.
b. He screamed so loud you could hear him in the next state.

MARCUS: It was so quiet.
JOHN: How quiet was it?

MARCUS: a. It was so quiet you could hear the grass growing.
b. It was so quiet no one was talking.

**Figurative Language**

# Activity 3—
# Completing Funny Exaggerations
## Answer Key

**(pgs 168–169)**

1. b
2. b
3. a
4. b
5. b
6. a
7. b
8. a

*Chapter 5: Humor*

# Activity 3—Completing Funny Exaggerations

## Extension Ideas

1. Have students explain why each Activity 3 exaggeration is funny. Explanations could be an oral or an extended writing activity.

2. Have students create their own exaggerated endings to the jokes provided in Activity 3. Challenge students to make up as many funny endings as they can.

**Figurative Language**

# Activity 4—Explaining Funny Stories

Name: _____ Date: _____

## Directions

Read the following funny stories. Then explain why each exaggeration or unusual situation is funny. Be prepared to discuss your answers. Ask questions if you need assistance.

**1** Teachers give us tests to find out what we know. The problem is, all of the questions on the tests are about things we don't know.

This is funny because: _____

_____

_____

**2** I didn't know anything before I started school. I still don't know anything, but now they test me on it.

This is funny because: _____

_____

_____

**3** My teacher said it is important to do something to help me relax before a big exam. So, in order to relax, I decided to take the next week off.

This is funny because: _____

_____

_____

**Figurative Language** © 2002 Thinking Publications
Duplication permitted for educational use only.

172

*Chapter 5: Humor*

**4**  Johnny asked his older sister, "Could you help me find the lowest common denominator for this math problem?" His sister replied, "I can't believe they haven't found it yet? I remember looking for it when I was your age!"

This is funny because: _____

_____

_____

**5**  My grandmother asked me to describe the food that is served in our school cafeteria. I replied, "Have you ever tasted dirty socks?"

This is funny because: _____

_____

_____

**6**  Our school dress code is simple: Anything that looks cool or that is comfortable is not allowed.

This is funny because: _____

_____

_____

**7**  I like recess so much that when I go to college, I may major in it.

This is funny because: _____

_____

_____

**8**  Teachers are supposed to be smart; after all, they went to college. So why do all of their textbooks have the answers in them?

This is funny because: _____

_____

_____

**Figurative Language** © 2002 Thinking Publications
Duplication permitted for educational use only.

**Figurative Language**

# Activity 4— Explaining Funny Stories
## Extension Ideas

1. Have students locate and bring in appropriate funny stories from newspapers, magazines, books, and online sources (e.g., *http://www.kidsjokes.co.uk*). Request them to read their stories to the group and explain the humor.

2. Provide students with captionless cartoon strips (use either cartoons without captions or use liquid correction fluid to remove the captions). Request students to add appropriate captions or to make up a funny story to go along with the pictures.

*Chapter 5: Humor*

# Activity 5—Humor Card Game

### Directions

Create a riddles and jokes card deck. Choose from the riddles and jokes provided below, or use other appropriate humor. Write each riddle or joke on one side of a 3" × 5" index card. If possible, have students help create the card deck.

Group students into two teams. Place the deck facedown in the center of a table. Have teams take turns choosing the top card from the deck and reading the joke aloud to the other team. The responding team must then explain what makes the riddle or joke humorous. If the responding team is successful, they keep the card. If the responding team is not successful, the card should be returned to the bottom of the deck. The team with the most cards at the end wins.

NOTE: As another option, write the questions or lead-ins to the riddles and jokes on one set of cards and the answers or punchlines on another set of cards. Then use the two decks to play a classic game of Memory by having students match the questions or lead-ins to the answers or punchlines.)

## Riddles

1. **Q.** Why did the woman take a bath with her shirt on?
   **A.** The label said "wash and wear."

2. **Q.** How do you make a band stand?
   **A.** Take away their chairs.

3. **Q.** What does a cat eat for breakfast?
   **A.** Mice Crispies.

4. **Q.** What do you call a bee that drops things?
   **A.** A fumble bee.

5. **Q.** What do you get when you cross a chicken with a desert?
   **A.** Fried chicken.

**Figurative Language**

6. **Q.** Why did the turkey eat so fast?

   **A.** He was a gobbler.

7. **Q.** What goes up and never comes down?

   **A.** Your age.

8. **Q.** Why did the hot dog shiver?

   **A.** It was covered with chili beans.

9. **Q.** What kind of tables do people eat?

   **A.** Vegetables.

10. **Q.** Why did the chicken cross the book?

    **A.** The get to the author side.

11. **Q.** Why does the Statue of Liberty stand in New York Harbor?

    **A.** Because she can't sit down.

12. **Q.** How do amoebas talk to each other?

    **A.** With their cell phones.

13. **Q.** What kind of cheese doesn't belong to you?

    **A.** Nacho cheese.

14. **Q.** What kind of bug is a musical bug?

    **A.** A humbug.

15. **Q.** Where do bunnies catch the bus?

    **A.** At the bus hop.

16. **Q.** What do you get when you cross snow with a tiger?

    **A.** Frostbite.


## Jokes

1. **THOMAS:** Where can you find elephants?

   **JUAN:** Anywhere. They're hard to hide.

2. **LAURA:** Can you tell me how long pot roast should be cooked?

   **TAMARA:** The same as short pot roast.

3. **LIBRARIAN:** Did you enjoy reading *The Hunchback of Notre Dame?*

   **STUDENT:** No, I read the first 100 pages, then I realized it wasn't about football.

176

*Chapter 5: Humor*

4. **TEACHER:** Shannon, give me a sentence that is a question.

   **SHANNON:** Why do I get all the hard ones?

   **TEACHER:** Very good.

5. **JODI:** Are we having burgers on the grill tonight?

   **MOM:** No, I think they're easier to eat on plates!

6. **STUDENT:** Is there life after death?

   **TEACHER:** Why do you ask?

   **STUDENT:** I may need the extra time to finish all this homework you gave us.

7. **JASON:** Would you ever yell at me for something I didn't do?

   **DAD:** Of course not. Why do you ask?

   **JASON:** Well, I didn't study for my test today.

8. **NATALIA:** How do they keep flies out of the cafeteria?

   **CHEN:** I don't know. How do they keep flies out of the cafeteria?

   **NATALIA:** Let them taste the food.

9. **SAM:** We never have any food fights in our cafeteria.

   **PAM:** Why, because it makes a mess?

   **SAM:** No, because someone might accidentally swallow the food.

10. **DANIEL:** The moon doesn't look hungry tonight.

    **DEBBIE:** How can you tell?

    **DANIEL:** Because it's full!

11. **DARRYL:** Every morning I dream that I'm falling from a 15-story building, but just before I hit the ground, I wake up.

    **SHERYL:** That's awful. What are you going to do about it?

    **DARRYL:** Start dreaming about a 20-story building. I need more sleep!

12. **CUSTOMER:** I'd like to try on that dress in the window.

    **CLERK:** I'm sorry, but you'll have to change in the dressing room like everyone else.

13. **CARLOS:** I'm so hungry.

    **JUANITA:** How hungry are you?

    **CARLOS:** I'm so hungry I could eat a horse.

14. **COLIN:** I'm so hot.

    **QUINN:** How hot are you?

    **COLIN:** I'm so hot you could fry an egg on my head.

177

**Figurative Language**

15.     **TIM:** The fog was so thick.

    **JIM:** How thick was it?

    **TIM:** It was so thick I could cut it with a knife.

16.   **MARIE:** Jamie is so thin.

    **BARRY:** How thin is she?

  **MARIE:** She's so thin you could slide her under the door.

17. **MICHAEL:** I was so mad.

    **MAX:** How mad were you?

  **MICHAEL:** I was so mad steam came pouring out of my ears.

18.     **PHIL:** I stood in line so long.

   **MIMI:** How long did you stand in line?

    **PHIL:** I stood in line so long I had another birthday.

19.    **GAIL:** He screamed so loud.

 **STEVEN:** How loud did he scream?

   **GAIL:** He screamed so loud you could hear him in the next state.

20. **MARCUS:** It was so quiet.

   **JOHN:** How quiet was it?

 **MARCUS:** It was so quiet you could hear the grass growing.

# Clichés and Slang

## Chapter 6

# What Are Slang and Clichés?

*Slang* refers to casual language that is used by a particular group to facilitate the exchange of information and to separate the "insiders" from the "outsiders" of the group. This form of figurative language is not considered appropriate conversation in polite company, and is rarely used in formal communication (Spears, 1982). Slang often references subjects that are considered taboo (e.g., sex, bodily functions, or alcohol and drug use), but in general, slang is an alternative way of saying something that often uses some kind of wordplay (e.g., calling McDonald's restaurant *Mickey D's*) (Spears, 1989). Adolescents often develop their own specialized set of slang terms so that they may be included in a particular social group. This specialized vocabulary sets them apart from the children they were and the adults they will become (Hyde, 1982). In fact, Donahue and Bryan (1984) indicated that in-group language is called *slang* when used by adolescents, but considered *jargon* when used by working professionals. Finally, Spears (1982) suggests that slang can serve to channel aggression, establish and maintain rank, and affirm virility in male groups.

There is no standard way to determine what is cliché, what is slang, and what is neither (Spears, 1989). Depending on the source, these terms may be interchanged. Clichés are expressions that are used so frequently that they become part of a language's lexicon. They may appear as a word, a phrase, or a complete sentence. They may also appear as a metaphor, a simile, an idiom, or a proverb. These figures of speech include fad words that usually have a short life, but if they persist and are widespread, they become standard American English (e.g., referring to a shy person as being *as quiet as a mouse*) (Spears, 1989). The popularity and use of clichés may wane, and sometimes they may even emerge years later and become common again.

179

**Figurative Language**

Advertising campaigns have introduced many clichés into the American lexicon. For example, the question *Where's the beef?* was initially used in an advertisement for Wendy's hamburgers, but soon people were using the expression in everyday conversations as a query when their expectation was that there was to be something more than what was presented to them. This example illustrates the figurative nature that clichés can embody and the significance they can take on in daily communication.

Even though slang and clichés are considered inappropriate in so many communication contexts, they are included in the figurative language types targeted in this book for several reasons. First, students need to be aware of appropriate and inappropriate uses of language. If inappropriate uses are not identified and appropriate alternatives are not generated, students will continue to use inappropriate forms. Second, the major part of American communication in movies, television, radio, newspapers, magazines, and informal conversation includes slang and clichés (Spears, 1989). If students are to survive in the "real" communication world, they must comprehend slang and clichés.

# Review of the Literature

Relatively little research exists in the area of slang and clichés. However, the cultural and social importance of slang—especially to adolescents—and the presence of clichés in society is obvious.

Slang is nothing new. It has been around in various forms for hundreds of years (Spears, 1982). What is under constant change and revision, however, is its usage. Among adolescents, what is popular in one regional area may spread into wider use among other adolescent groups across the country. For example, in the 1980s, slang used by Californian "valley girls," such as *gag me with a spoon,* soon spread and was used throughout the United States, especially with the attention given to such language by the entertainment industry. Music, music videos, and television programming directed toward adolescent audiences frequently uses and perpetuates the current slang being spoken by teenagers. Adolescents with language disorders can be ostracized from a group they wish to belong to due to their difficulty understanding and using popular slang expressions (Larson and McKinley, 1995).

Clichés can bore, irritate, or unintentionally amuse a listener or reader. Clichés are used more frequently in spoken form and are seen as a sort of verbal shorthand for common ideas. Thus, when spoken, rather than written, clichés are considered more acceptable. However, Lunsford and Connors (1989) warn that spoken clichés can sound insincere and should not be overused. The use of clichés in writing is often considered immature and ineffective, as clichés do not add depth or interest to what is written, and their use typically signals an unskilled writer. Adolescents and adults who struggle with figurative language forms may overuse clichés, use them inappropriately, and/or misunderstand their use. Because adolescents with language disorders have difficulty understanding

180

*Chapter 6: Clichés and Slang*

and using all forms of figurative language (Larson and McKinley, 1995), their understanding and use of clichés is undoubtedly lacking.

# Developmental Information

Since little research has been conducted in the areas of slang and clichés, little can be said related to the typical development of these forms of figurative language. However, since clichés are simply overused metaphors, similes, idioms, and proverbs, the development of clichés can be gleaned from the development of these other forms of figurative language. Refer to Chapters 2, 3, and 4 for discussions related to the development of metaphors, similes, idioms, and proverbs.

Donahue and Bryan (1984) underscore the importance of slang usage, saying, "perhaps in no other developmental phase is the relationship between communication skills and peer group membership as apparent as in adolescence" (p. 11). As adolescents attempt to fit in with their peers, using and understanding slang is critical. Furthermore, as adults in the working world, many will need to develop and use the specialized jargon that is vital to communicating with fellow employees in a particular profession.

# How Can This Chapter Be Used?

There are five activities in Chapter 6 and no particular hierarchy to the presentation of the activity types. Feel free to choose which activities to use and in which order. It is recommended that the card game described in Activity 5 be conducted after students have been exposed to the preceding activities within the chapter. Survey a few students with typical development to become familiar with current slang being used by adolescents. Add or eliminate slang items to the activities, as appropriate, before beginning each activity. It may be helpful to have a slang and cliché dictionary available for student use.

- **Activity 1** targets understanding of slang through a multiple-choice task. One form is provided for Activity 1, as is an answer key and extension ideas.

- **Activity 2** requires students to interpret slang from the past by equating it with more current slang. The activity uses an open-ended response format and includes one form and extension ideas.

- **Activity 3** challenges students to demonstrate their understanding of common clichés using a multiple-choice format. One form is provided for Activity 3, along with an answer key and extension ideas.

- **Activity 4** directs students to change sentences containing clichés so that they do not contain clichés. This activity includes Form A and Form B, plus extension ideas.

181

**Figurative Language**

- **Activity 5** presents directions and a list of slang and clichés for creating a card game to target understanding and use of these expressions. (Also, consider using appropriate slang and clichés from students' daily lives for this activity.)

For all five activities, encourage students to talk about the possible meanings of each slang and cliché expression as the tasks are discussed and completed. Also, direct students to read the tasks aloud to help them better recognize whether their response is accurate. Help students understand how to use context cues and reference materials (e.g., a slang dictionary) in order to figure out the meanings of these expressions. Refer to "Suggested Adaptations" (page 7) for optional reading and writing adaptations.

Consider these activity pages as lesson or discussion guides rather than as paper-and-pencil tasks. Bridge discussions by talking about when students might encounter the given slang and clichés in their academic and/or personal lives.

---

### A Word of Caution

Because of the controversial nature of some slang and clichés, carefully select appropriate targets. As with the topic of humor in Chapter 5, figures of speech considered offensive or in poor taste should be avoided. Class rules and limits need to be established before beginning this chapter. You may also need to inform parents and appropriate school staff of the purpose of covering this form of figurative language and the class rules and limits for the activities in this chapter. Careful planning will ensure that the activities are fully enjoyed by all students. The slang and clichés used in the activities in this chapter are considered neutral and unoffensive. Still, double-check each activity and eliminate any figures of speech that may cause a problem.

---

182

*Chapter 6: Clichés and Slang*

# Activity 1—Understanding Slang

Name: _____   Date: _____

**Directions**

*Slang* refers to words and expressions used by a particular group of people to mean something different than the expected definition. Read each set of sentences below. Notice the slang expressions are in bold letters. For each item, circle the letter of the the answer that means the same as the sentence containing the slang. Be prepared to discuss your answers. Ask questions if you need assistance.

1. I'm going to my **crib**. I'm gonna play some video games and **raid the fridge.**

    a. I'm going home to play video games and get a snack from the refrigerator.

    b. I'm going to put the baby in its bed and go and get her a bottle out of the refrigerator.

2. Quit **flossin'** me. I know you took that money. You'd better hand it over or we're **gonna scrap!**

    a. Stop laughing at me. I know you took that money. You'd better give me my cash or we're going to have some material left over.

    b. Stop lying to me. I know you took that money. You'd better give it to me or we're gonna have a fight!

3. He must have some **serious flow** to be in **a ride** like that!

    a. He must have a lot of money to drive a car like that!

    b. He must have a lot of water to be in a boat like that!

**Figurative Language** © 2002 Thinking Publications
Duplication permitted for educational use only.

183

**Figurative Language**

4. She just got some **fresh rags** and now she's **really fly!**

   a. She got some new dust rags and now she can clean her room really fast!

   b. She got some new clothes and now she's really good looking!

5. Those are my **peeps** and you'll never see me **dis** them.

   a. Those are my friends and you'll never see me disrespect them.

   b. Those are my parents and you'll never see me disturb them.

6. I'm gonna run to **Mickey D's** and **toss chow** before I go to work.

   a. I'm going to run to McDonald's and eat quickly before I go to work.

   b. I'm going to run to Disney World and throw around some money before I go to work.

7. This place is really **jammin'**. I haven't been to a party this **thick** in months.

   a. This place is really busy. I haven't been to a party this good in months.

   b. This place is really loud. I haven't been to a party this awful in months.

8. Well, **duh!** I can't believe I said that in front of a teacher. **My bad!**

   a. Well, how funny! I can't believe I said that in front of a teacher. My goodness!

   b. Well, how stupid of me! I can't believe I said that in front of a teacher. My mistake!

9. That movie was **the bomb.** Now I need to head home and **catch some Zs.**

   a. That movie was awful. Now I need to head home and do my English report.

   b. That movie was great. Now I need to head home and get some sleep.

10. He's in big trouble. The **five-o** found out that he **splacked** a car.

   a. He's in big trouble. The police found out that he stole a car.

   b. He's in big trouble. His parents found out that he got into a car accident.

*Figurative Language* © 2002 Thinking Publications
Duplication permitted for educational use only.

184

*Chapter 6: Clichés and Slang*

# Activity 1—Understanding Slang
## Answer Key

**(pgs 183–184)**

1. a
2. b
3. a
4. b
5. a
6. a
7. a
8. b
9. b
10. a

**Figurative Language**

# Activity 1— Understanding Slang
## Extension Ideas

1. Have students write appropriate examples of their own slang. For each example, direct students to also write the actual meaning of the slang. Then have students share their examples with the group.

2. Have students locate and bring in examples of appropriate slang they find in media sources (e.g., online, in magazine ads, and on TV). Have students present the slang examples orally or in written form and offer literal interpretations of the slang.

*Chapter 6: Clichés and Slang*

# Activity 2—Interpreting Yesterday's Slang

Name: _____  Date: _____

## Directions

Slang expressions come and go. The slang expressions listed below were popular a number of years ago. Read each expression and think of a way to say the same thing using today's slang. Write your answer on the blank provided. An example has been completed to get you started. Be prepared to discuss your answers. Ask questions if you need assistance.

---

**Example**

It costs $500 a month to rent my **pad.** *(pad* = house or apartment)

Today's slang: *It costs $500 a month to rent my crib.*

---

**1** **All systems are a go** for the party. *(all systems are a go* = everything is ready)

Today's slang: _____

_____

**2** That music is **all the rage.** *(all the rage* = very popular)

Today's slang: _____

_____

**3** She is constantly **bad-mouthing** her friends.

*(bad-mouthing* = saying mean things about someone or something)

Today's slang: _____

_____

*Figurative Language* © 2002 Thinking Publications
Duplication permitted for educational use only.

187

**Figurative Language**

**4**  That kid is a **ball of fire.** *(ball of fire* = a very active and energetic person)

Today's slang: _____

_____

**5**  She was acting like a **cold fish.** *(cold fish* = an aloof or standoffish person)

Today's slang: _____

_____

**6**  He was a **dead duck.** *(dead duck* = someone doomed to failure)

Today's slang: _____

_____

**7**  The squirrel sitting in the road was **a goner.**
*(a goner* = someone or something that is doomed)

Today's slang: _____

_____

**8**  My sister paid me back, so we were **even-steven.** *(even-steven* = equal)

Today's slang: _____

_____

**9**  My dad **flipped out** when he saw the telephone bill. *(flipped out* = lost control)

Today's slang: _____

_____

**10**  The teacher told us to **cool it.** *(cool it* = calm down)

Today's slang: _____

_____

**Figurative Language** © 2002 Thinking Publications
Duplication permitted for educational use only.

188

# Activity 2— Interpreting Yesterday's Slang

## Extension Ideas

1. Have students interview family members (such as parents and grandparents) about their use of slang when they were younger. Encourage students to write down examples of slang from the past and bring them in to share with the class. Have students guess the literal meanings of the various slang expressions.

2. Use a slang dictionary to create a list of past and present slang expressions. Have students match expressions with similar meanings.

**Figurative Language**

# Activity 3—Understanding Clichés

Name: _____    Date: _____

## Directions

*Cliché* refers to an expression that is used so much that it develops an accepted meaning. Read each set of sentences. Notice that the cliché is in bold letters. For each item, circle the letter of the answer that means the same as the sentence containing the cliché. Be prepared to discuss your answers. Ask questions if you need assistance.

**1** Anthony doesn't know when to stop teasing. He just keeps **adding insult to injury.**

*Adding insult to injury* means:

a. Making a bad situation worse

b. Punching someone and making him or her bleed

**2** **After all is said and done,** I'll probably look back at this and laugh.

*After all is said and done* means:

a. When everyone stops talking

b. Finally, after everything is concluded

**3** If you **aid and abet** someone, you could go to jail too—even if you didn't actually commit the crime yourself.

*Aid and abet* means:

a. To help someone do something wrong

b. To place a bet in a card game

**4** To this year's Senior Class prom I say, **all's well that ends well.**

*All's well that ends well* means:

a. If the ending was good, the event was fine

b. That was the last prom we will ever have at this school

**Figurative Language** © 2002 Thinking Publications
Duplication permitted for educational use only.

190

Chapter 6: Clichés and Slang

The soldiers were **armed to the teeth** and no match for the guerrilla forces.

*Armed to the teeth* means:

a. They were having their teeth fixed

b. They were heavily equipped with weapons

After our lunch break, it's **back to the salt mines.**

*Back to the salt mines* means:

a. It's time to get back to work

b. The lunch was too salty

Stop **beating a dead horse.** I'm tired of hearing your excuses about this matter.

*Beating a dead horse* means:

a. Continuing to argue after a point has been made

b. Being cruel to animals, such as horses

I'd rather go to a small college than a large university. I want to be **a big fish in a little pond.**

*A big fish in a little pond* means:

a. To be a fisherman in college

b. To be an important person in a smaller group of people

Sometimes buying something off of the Web is like buying **a pig in a poke.**

*A pig in a poke* means:

a. Something offered that conceals its true value

b. Ham sold on the Web

**10** That batch of fudge is the **cream of the crop.**

*Cream of the crop* means:

a. Made of milk

b. Best of all

**Figurative Language** © 2002 Thinking Publications
Duplication permitted for educational use only.

191

**Figurative Language**

# Activity 3—Understanding Clichés
## Answer Key

**(pgs 190–191)**

1. a
2. b
3. a
4. a
5. b
6. a
7. a
8. b
9. a
10. b

*Chapter 6: Clichés and Slang*

# Activity 3— Understanding Clichés

## Extension Ideas

1. Have students use at least five clichés while writing an extended paragraph. Then have them rewrite their paragraphs, changing the clichés into a less-familiar way of saying the same thing. See the examples below.

### Paragraph with Clichés

*Like clockwork, my little sister started bothering me while I was doing my homework last night. She was happy as a clam, but I needed to get back to the salt mines since I had a big report to finish. To add insult to injury, my computer kept locking up and I couldn't get my printer to work. After all was said and done, I did get my report finished because my mom fixed my computer and put my sister to bed.*

### Paragraph Translated without Clichés

*Just like always, my little sister started bothering me while I was doing my homework last night. She was very pleased to be pestering me, but I needed to get back to work since I had a big report to finish. Unfortunately, my computer kept locking up and I couldn't get my printer to work. Finally, I did get my report finished because my mom fixed my computer and put my sister to bed.*

2. Have students complete 3" × 5" index cards writing the following on each card:

   - a cliche
   - the meaning of the cliché
   - a sentence containing the cliché

   Consider awarding a bonus point for each card completed and turned in. Keep a collection of the cards in alphabetical order to use as a class cliché dictionary.

193

**Figurative Language**

# Activity 4—Creating Alternative Sentences
## Form A

Name: _____  Date: _____

| **Directions** |
| --- |
| Read the following sentences that contain clichés in bold letters. Then write your own sentence that means the same as the sentence provided, without using a cliché. Be prepared to discuss your answers. Ask questions if you need assistance. |

**1** The math class I took last semester was **as easy as pie.**

Your sentence: _____

_____

_____

**2** The kids I babysat for last night were **as good as gold.**

Your sentence: _____

_____

_____

**3** Jade has always been a cute kid; her dad says she's **as pretty as a picture.**

Your sentence: _____

_____

_____

**Figurative Language** © 2002 Thinking Publications
Duplication permitted for educational use only.

*Chapter 6: Clichés and Slang*

**4** My mom was **as proud as a peacock** when she won first prize in a contest.

Your sentence: _____

_____

_____

**5** Sam finished his dinner **as quick as a wink.**

Your sentence: _____

_____

_____

**6** Gabriella almost never spoke in class; she was **as quiet as a mouse.**

Your sentence: _____

_____

_____

**7** When the parents called home, the babysitter said everything was **as right as rain.**

Your sentence: _____

_____

_____

**8** Nina worked hard, but she was still **as poor as a church mouse.**

Your sentence: _____

_____

_____

**Figurative Language** © 2002 Thinking Publications
Duplication permitted for educational use only.

195

**Figurative Language**

# Activity 4—Creating Alternative Sentences
## Form B

Name: _____ Date: _____

| Directions |
| --- |
| Read the following sentences that contain clichés in bold letters. Then write your own sentence that means the same as the sentence provided, without using a cliché. Be prepared to discuss your answers. Ask questions if you need assistance. |

**1** Deandre was **as happy as a clam** when she got chocolate cake for her birthday.

Your sentence: _____

_____

_____

**2** Dependable employees are **scarcer than hens' teeth.**

Your sentence: _____

_____

_____

**3** The mail carrier showed up **like clockwork** every day.

Your sentence: _____

_____

_____

**Figurative Language** © 2002 Thinking Publications
Duplication permitted for educational use only.

196

*Chapter 6: Clichés and Slang*

**4** Davis got **as sick as a dog** after eating his tenth slice of pizza.

Your sentence: _____

_____

_____

**5** Giovanni was **as stubborn as a mule** when it came to cleaning his room.

Your sentence: _____

_____

_____

**6** Meg was **as busy as a bee** with preparations for the neighborhood picnic.

Your sentence: _____

_____

_____

**7** The fog was **as thick as pea soup** this morning.

Your sentence: _____

_____

_____

**8** Mickaela's shirt was **as white as the driven snow.**

Your sentence: _____

_____

_____

**Figurative Language** © 2002 Thinking Publications
Duplication permitted for educational use only.

197

**Figurative Language**

# Activity 4—Creating Alternative Sentences

## Extension Ideas

1. Have students underline or highlight the words in each Activity 4 sentence that give clues to the literal meanings of the clichés. Ask students to explain their choices.

2. Challenge students to create a second and third sentence for each sentence in Activity 3 and Activity 4 that contains a cliché.

# Activity 5— Clichés and Slang Card Game

## Directions

Create a slang and/or clichés card deck. Choose from the examples provided below or use appropriate slang and clichés from students' daily lives. For each slang expression or cliché, write the expression on one side of a 3" × 5" index card and the meaning on the other side of the card. If possible, have students help create the card deck.

Group students into two teams. Place the deck with the meanings facedown in the center of a table. Have teams take turns choosing the top card from the deck and saying the slang or cliché expression aloud to the other team. The responding team must then state the meaning of the given expression. If the responding team is successful, they keep the card. If the responding team is not successful, the card should be returned to the bottom of the deck. The team with the most cards at the end wins.

NOTE: As another option, write slang or cliché expressions on one set of cards and their meanings on another set of cards. Then use the two decks to play a classic game of Memory by having students match the expressions to their meanings.

| Slang Expression | Meaning |
| --- | --- |
| crib | home |
| raid the fridge | get food from the refrigerator |
| flossin' | lying |
| gonna scrap | going to fight |
| serious flow | a lot of money |
| a ride | a car |
| fresh rags | new clothes |
| really fly | really good looking |
| peeps | friends |
| dis | to disrespect |
| Mickey D's | McDonald's |

**Figurative Language**

| Slang Expression | Meaning |
| --- | --- |
| toss chow | eat quickly |
| jammin' | lively and busy |
| thick | great |
| duh | how stupid |
| my bad | my mistake |
| the bomb | terrific |
| catch some Zs | get some sleep |
| five-o | police |
| splacked a car | stole a car |
| all systems are a go | everything is ready |
| all the rage | very popular |
| bad-mouthing | saying mean things about someone or something |
| ball of fire | a very active and energetic person |
| cold fish | an aloof or standoffish person |
| dead duck | someone doomed to failure |
| a goner | someone or something that is doomed |
| even-steven | equal |
| flipped out | lost control |
| cool it | calm down |

| Cliché | Meaning |
| --- | --- |
| adding insult to injury | making a bad situation worse |
| after all is said and done | finally, after everything is concluded |
| aid and abet | to help someone do something wrong |
| all's well that ends well | if the ending was good, the event was fine |
| armed to the teeth | heavily equipped with weapons |
| back to the salt mines | back to work |
| beating a dead horse | continuing to argue after a point has been made |
| a big fish in a little pond | an important person in a smaller group of people |
| a pig in a poke | something offered that conceals its true value |
| cream of the crop | best of all |
| as easy as pie | very easy |
| as good as gold | in perfect condition or behaving wonderfully |
| as pretty as a picture | very beautiful |
| as proud as a peacock | highly honored and proud |

*Chapter 6: Clichés and Slang*

| Cliché | Meaning |
| --- | --- |
| as quick as a wink | very fast |
| as quiet as a mouse | very quiet and shy |
| as right as rain | everything is just fine |
| as poor as a church mouse | extremely poor |
| as happy as a clam | extremely happy |
| scarcer than hen's teeth | difficult to find or nonexistent |
| like clockwork | regularly scheduled |
| as sick as a dog | very ill |
| as stubborn as a mule | very stubborn and difficult to deal with |
| as busy as a bee | extremely busy |
| as thick as pea soup | very dense and concentrated |
| as white as the driven snow | pure white |

# References

Ackerman, B.P. (1982). On comprehending idioms: Do children get the picture? *Journal of Experimental Psychology, 33,* 439–454.

Arnold, K.M., and Hornett, D. (1990). Teaching idioms to children who are deaf. *Teaching Exceptional Children, 22,* 14–17.

Asch, S.E., and Nerlove, H. (1960). The development of double function terms in children. In B. Kaplan and S. Wapner (Eds.), *Perspectives in psychology* (pp. 47–60). New York: International Universities Press.

Baechle, C.L., and Lian, M.G. (1990). The effects of direct feedback and practice on metaphor performance in children with learning disabilities. *Journal of Learning Disabilities, 23,* 451–455.

Bernstein, D.K. (1986). The development of humor: Implications for assessment and intervention. *Topics in Language Disorders, 6*(4), 65–72.

Billow, R. (1975). A cognitive developmental study of metaphor comprehension. *Developmental Psychology, 11,* 415–423.

Billow, R. (1977). Metaphor: A review of the psychological literature. *Psychological Bulletin, 84,* 81–92.

Boatner, M.T., and Gates, J.E. (1975). *A dictionary of American idioms.* Woodbury, NY: Barron's Educational Series.

Britton, B.K. (1978). Lexical ambiguity of words in English text. *Behavior Research Methods and Instrumentation, 10,* 1–7.

Brinton, B., Fujiki, M., and Mackey, T. (1985). Elementary school age children's comprehension of specific idiomatic expressions. *Journal of Communication Disorders, 18,* 245–257.

Bryant, J., and Zillmann, D. (1989). Using humor to promote learning in the classroom. *Journal of Children in Contemporary Society, 20,* 49–78.

Cacciari, C., and Levorato, M. (1989). How children understand idioms in discourse. *Journal of Child Language, 16,* 387–405.

Dahany, M. (1986). On the metaphorical language of L2 research. *Modern Language Journal, 70,* 228–235.

Dedrick, S., and Lattyak, J. (1984). *Many meanings.* Beaverton, OR: Dormac.

Donahue, M., and Bryan, T. (1984). Communication skills and peer relations of learning disabled adolescents. *Topics in Language Disorders, 4*(2), 10–12.

Douglas, J.D., and Peel, B. (1979). The development of metaphor and proverb translation in children grades 1 through 7. *Journal of Educational Research, 73,* 116–119.

Durkin, K., and Manning, J. (1989). Polysemy and the subjective lexicon: Semantic relatedness and the salience of intraword senses. *Journal of Psycholinguistic Research, 18,* 577–612.

Evans, M., and Gamble, D. (1988). Attribute saliency and metaphor interpretation in school-age children. *Journal of Child Language, 15,* 435–449.

**Figurative Language**

Ezell, H., and Goldstein, H. (1992). Teaching idiom comprehension to children with mental retardation. *Journal of Applied Behavior Analysis, 25,* 181–191.

Fowles, B., and Glanz, M.E. (1977). Competence and talent in verbal riddle comprehension. *Journal of Child Language, 4,* 433–452.

Fry, E. (1977). Fry's readability graph: Clarifications, validity, and extension to level 17. *Journal of Reading, 21,* 242–251.

Fry, E., Kress, J., and Fountoukidis, D. (1993). *The reading teacher's book of lists* (3rd ed.). Englewood Cliffs, NJ: Prentice Hall.

Gardner, H., Kircher, M., Winner, E., and Perkins, D. (1975). Children's metaphoric productions and preferences. *Journal of Child Language, 2,* 125–141.

Gardner, H., Winner, E., Bechhofer, R., and Wolf, D. (1978). The development of figurative language. In K.E. Nelson (Ed.), *Children's language* (pp. 1–38). New York: Gardner Press.

Gibbs, R.W. (1986). Skating on thin ice: Literal meaning and understanding in conversation. *Discourse Processes, 9,* 17–30.

Gibbs, R.W. (1991). Semantic analyzability in children's understanding of idioms. *Journal of Speech and Hearing Research, 34,* 613–620.

Gorham, D.R. (1956). A proverbs test for clinical and experimental use. *Psychological Reports, 2,* 1–12.

Hirsch, E.D., Kett, J.F., and Trefil, J. (1988). *The dictionary of cultural literacy.* Boston: Houghton Mifflin.

Hirsh-Pasek, K., Gleitman, L., and Gleitman, H. (1978). What did the brain say to the mind? A study of the detection and report of ambiguity by young children. In A. Sinclair, O. Jarvella, and W. Levelt (Eds.), *A child's conception of language* (pp. 97–132). New York: Springer-Verlag.

Honeck, R., Sowry, B., and Voegtle, K. (1978). Proverbial understanding in a pictorial context. *Child Development, 49,* 327–331.

Hyde, J. (1982, March). Rat talk: The special vocabulary of some teenagers. *English Journal,* 98–101.

Iran-Nejad, A., Ortony, A., and Rittenhouse, R. (1981). The comprehension of metaphorical uses of English by deaf children. *Journal of Speech and Hearing Research, 24,* 551–556.

Irujo, S. (1986). A piece of cake: Learning and teaching idioms. *English Language Teaching Journal, 40,* 236–242.

Johnson, C., Ionson, M., and Torreiter, S. (1997). Assessing children's knowledge of multiple meaning words. *American Journal of Speech-Language Pathology, 6*(1), 77–86.

Johnson, D., and Pearson, P. (1984). *Teaching reading vocabulary* (2nd ed.). New York: Holt, Rinehart, and Winston.

Jones, J., and Stone, C.A. (1989). Metaphor comprehension by language learning disabled and normally achieving adolescent boys. *Learning Disability Quarterly, 12,* 251–260.

Kutner, N. (1988, April 14). Different ages find different things funny. *Sun-Sentinel,* p. 3.

204

Larson, Vicki Lord, and McKinley, N. (1995). *Language disorders in older students: Preadolescents and adolescents.* Eau Claire, WI: Thinking Publications.

Lazar, R.T., Warr-Leeper, G.A., Beel-Nicholson, C., and Johnson, S. (1989). Elementary school teachers' use of multiple meaning expressions. *Language, Speech, and Hearing Services in Schools, 20,* 420–430.

Lee, R.F., and Kamhi, A.G. (1990). Metaphoric competence in children with learning disabilities. *Journal of Learning Disabilities, 23,* 476–482.

Levorato, M.C., and Cacciari, C. (1992). Children's comprehension and production of idioms: The role of context and familiarity. *Journal of Child Language, 19,* 415–433.

Lodge, D.N., and Leach, E.A. (1975). Children's acquisition of idioms in the English language. *Journal of Speech and Hearing Research, 18,* 521–529.

Lund, N.J., and Duchan, J.F. (1988). *Assessing children's language in naturalistic contexts* (2nd ed.). Englewood Cliffs, NJ: Prentice Hall.

Lunsford, A., and Connors, R. (1989). *The St. Martin's handbook.* New York: St. Martin's Press.

Mason, J., Kniseley, E., and Kendall, J. (1979). Effects of polysemous words on sentence comprehension. *Reading Research Quarterly, 1,* 49–65.

May, A.B. (1979). All the angles of idiom instruction. *The Reading Teacher, 32,* 680–682.

McGhee, P. (1971a). Cognitive development and children's comprehension of humor. *Child Development, 42,* 123–138.

McGhee, P. (1971b). Development of the humor response: A review of the literature. *Psychological Bulletin, 76,* 328–348.

McGhee, P. (1971c). The role of operational thinking in children's humor. *Child Development, 42,* 733–744.

McGhee, P., and Chapman, A. (Eds.). (1980). *Children's humor.* New York: Wiley.

Nippold, M.A. (1985). Comprehension of figurative language in youth. *Topics in Language Disorders, 5*(3), 1–20.

Nippold, M.A. (1991). Evaluating and enhancing idiom comprehension in language-disordered students. *Language, Speech, and Hearing Services in Schools, 22,* 100–106.

Nippold, M.A. (1998). *Later language development: The school-age and adolescent years* (2nd ed.). Austin, TX: Pro-Ed.

Nippold, M.A., Allen, M.M., and Kirsch, D.I. (2000). How adolescents comprehend unfamiliar proverbs: The role of top-down and bottom-up processes. *Journal of Speech, Language, and Hearing Research, 43,* 621–630.

Nippold, M.A., Allen, M.M., and Kirsch, D.I. (2001). Proverb comprehension as a function of reading proficiency in preadolescents. *Language, Speech, and Hearing Services in Schools, 32,* 90–111.

Nippold, M.A., Cuyler, J.S., and Braunbeck-Price, R. (1988). Explanation of ambiguous advertisements: A developmental study with children and adolescents. *Journal of Speech and Hearing Research, 31,* 466–474.

**Figurative Language**

Nippold, M., and Haq, F.S. (1996). Proverb comprehension in youth: The role of concreteness and familiarity. *Journal of Speech and Hearing Research, 39,* 166–176.

Nippold, M., Leonard, L., and Kail, R. (1984). Syntactic and conceptual factors in children's understanding of metaphors. *Journal of Speech and Hearing Research, 27,* 197–205.

Nippold, M.A., Moran, C., and Schwarz, I.E. (2001). Idiom understanding in preadolescents: Synergy in action. *American Journal of Speech-Language Pathology, 10,* 169–180.

Nippold, M.A., and Rudzinski, M. (1993). Familiarity and transparency in idiom explanation: A developmental study of children and adolescents. *Journal of Speech and Hearing Research, 36,* 728–737.

Nippold, M.A., and Taylor, C.L. (1995). Idiom understanding in youth: Further examination of familiarity and transparency. *Journal of Speech and Hearing Research, 38,* 426–433.

Nippold, M.A., and Taylor, C.L. (1996). Idiom understanding in Australian youth: A cross-cultural comparison. *Journal of Speech and Hearing Research, 39,* 442–447.

Nippold, M.A., Uhden, L.D., and Schwarz, I.E. (1997). Proverb explanation through the lifespan: A developmental study of adolescents and adults. *Journal of Speech, Language, and Hearing Research, 40,* 245–253.

O'Brien, D.G., and Martin, M.A. (1988). Does figurative language present a unique comprehension problem? *Journal of Reading Behavior, 20,* 63–87.

Ortony, A., Turner, T., and Larson-Shapiro, N. (1985a). Cultural and instructional influences on figurative language comprehension by inner city children. *Research in the Teaching of English, 19*(1), 25–36.

Ortony, A., Turner, T., and Larson-Shapiro, N. (1985b). *Cultural and instructional influences on figurative language comprehension by inner city children* (Tech. Rep. No. 335). Urbana, IL: University Center for the Study of Reading.

Perret, G. (1991). *Super funny school jokes.* New York: Sterling.

Piaget, J. (1926). *The language and thought of the child.* (M. Worden, Trans.). New York: Harcourt, Brace, and World. (Original French edition published 1923)

Pollio, M., and Pollio, H. (1974). The development of figurative language in children. *Journal of Psycholinguistic Research, 3,* 185–201.

Pollio, M., and Pollio, H. (1979). A test of metaphoric comprehension: Preliminary data. *Journal of Child Language, 6,* 111–120.

Readence, J.E., Baldwin, R.S., and Rickelman, R.J. (1983). Word knowledge and metaphorical interpretation. *Research in the Teaching of English, 17,* 349–358.

Richardson, C., and Church, J. (1959). A developmental analysis of proverb interpretations. *Journal of Genetic Psychology, 94,* 169–179.

Schaefer, C.E. (1975). The importance of measuring metaphorical thinking. *Gifted Quarterly, 19,* 140–148.

Schultz, T. (1974). Development of the appreciation of riddles. *Child Development, 45,* 100–105.

Schultz, T., and Horibe, F. (1974). Development of the appreciation of verbal jokes. *Developmental Psychology, 10,* 13–20.

Seidenberg, P.L., and Bernstein, D.K. (1986). The comprehension of similes and metaphors by learning disabled and non-learning disabled children. *Language, Speech, and Hearing Services in Schools, 17,* 219–229.

Smith, M., Schloss, P.J., and Israelite, N.K. (1986). Evaluation of a simile recognition treatment program for hearing impaired students. *Journal of Speech and Hearing Disorders, 51,* 134–139.

Spears, R. (1982). *Slang and euphemism.* New York: David.

Spears, R. (1989). *Dictionary of American slang and colloquial expressions.* Lincolnwood, IL: National Textbook.

Spector, C.C. (1990). Linguistic humor comprehension of normal and language-impaired adolescents. *Journal of Speech and Hearing Disorders, 55,* 533–541.

Stahl, S.A., Richek, M.A., and Vandevier, R.J. (1990, November). *Learning meaning vocabulary through through listening: A sixth grade replication.* Paper presented at the annual National Reading Conference, Miami, FL.

Towne, R.L., and Entwisle, L.M. (1993). Metaphoric comprehension in adolescents with traumatic brain injury and in adolescents with language learning disability. *Language, Speech, and Hearing Services in Schools, 24,* 100–107.

Vosniadou, S. (1987). Children and metaphors. *Child Development, 58,* 870–885.

Watts, A. (1950). *The language of mental development.* London: Harrap.

Wiig, E. (1985). *Words, expressions, contexts: A figurative language program.* Columbus, OH: Merrill.

Wiig, E., and Semel, E. (1980). *Language assessment and intervention for the learning disabled.* Columbus, OH: Merrill.

Wiig, E., and Semel, E. (1984). *Language assessment and intervention for the learning disabled* (2nd ed.). Columbus, OH: Merrill.

Winner, E. (1979). New names for old things: The emergence of metaphoric language. *Journal of Child Language, 6,* 469–492.

Ziv, A. (1976). Facilitating effects of humor on creativity. *Journal of Educational Psychology, 68,* 318–322.